C000148683

HUTCHINSON

# Chronology of
# World Events

**Titles in this series**

# HUTCHINSON

## Chronology of
# World Events

BROCKHAMPTON PRESS
LONDON

Copyright © Helicon Publishing Ltd 1993
All rights reserved

Helicon Publishing Ltd
42 Hythe Bridge Street
Oxford OX1 2EP

Printed and bound in Great Britain by
Mackays of Chatham Plc,
Chatham, Kent

This edition published 1997 by
Brockhampton Press Ltd
20 Bloomsbury Street
London WC1B 3QA
(*a member of the Hodder Headline PLC Group*)

ISBN 1-86019-581-4

British Cataloguing in Publication Data

A catalogue record for this book is available
from the British Library

## BC

| | |
|---|---|
| *c. 4–3.5 million* | *Australopithecus*, the first hominid, appeared in E Africa. |
| *c. 2.5 million* | *Homo habilis* used stone tools in Africa. |
| *c. 1.7 million* | *Homo habilis* built first structured habitats. |
| *c. 1.5 million* | *Homo erectus* lived in E Africa. |
| *c. 500,000* | *Homo erectus* lived in China. |
| *c. 200,000* | *Homo sapiens* originated in Africa. |
| *c. 60,000–35,000* | Ice-age land bridge between Asia and Alaska allowed migration from Siberia to America. |
| *c. 50,000* | Modern humans in Asia. |
| *c. 40,000* | Probable arrival of modern humans in Australia. |
| *c. 35,000* | Modern humans in Europe. |
| *c. 30,000* | Tools in use in Japan. |
| *c. 26,000* | Ritual cremation in Australia. |
| *c. 23,000* | Modern humans in the Americas. |
| *c. 15,000* | Cave wall paintings made at Lascaux, France. |
| | Agriculture first practised in Egypt. |
| | Potterymaking. Jōmon culture began in Japan (to 300 BC). |
| *c. 9000* | South America settled by peoples from Central America. |
| *c. 8400* | Domesticated dogs in America. |
| *c. 8000* | Reed boats were developed in Mesopotamia and Egypt; dug-out canoes were used in NW Europe. |
| | Last glaciers melted in Britain and the climate warmed. |
| *c. 7500* | Goats and sheep domesticated in Middle East. |
| | First agriculture in SW Asia. |

| | |
|---|---|
| *c. 7000* | Walled settlement at Jericho. |
| *c. 6000* | First farming communities appeared in SE Europe. |
| | S Sweden inhabited. |
| *c. 5000* | Sumerians settled in Mesopotamia. |
| | Bronze Age began in the Middle East. |
| | Inuit people arrived in North America. |
| | Domestication of llamas in South America. |
| | Agriculture developed in Mexico. |
| | Rock and cave painting in Sahara. |
| *c. 4000* | Rice grown in China. |
| | Indus Valley became a population centre. |
| | Egyptians used single-masted square-rigged ships on the Nile. |
| *c. 3500* | Height of Sumerian civilization. |
| *c. 3200* | Beginnings of Egyptian religious drama. |
| *c. 3000* | Menes united Egypt. |
| | Semitic tribes occupied Assyria. |
| | Minoan civilization began in Crete. |
| | Athens first inhabited. |
| *c. 2800* | Beginning of Sage Kings period in China. |
| | Step pyramid built at Sakkara, Egypt. |
| | Stonehenge was constructed: first phase. |
| *c. 2650* | Great Pyramid built at Gîza in Egypt. |
| *c. 2600* | Egyptians retaliated for Palestinian attacks on trade caravans. |
| | Semitic peoples in Syria and N Africa. |
| | Maya civilization began in the Yucatán Peninsula. |

| | |
|---|---|
| *c. 2500* | Great Pyramids at Giza built. |
| | Indus Valley civilization began in India. |
| | Agriculture developed in South America. |
| | A positional numbering (place-value) system was developed in Mesopotamia. |
| *c. 2350* | Sargon founded Akkadian Empire. |
| *c. 2300* | Chinese astronomers made their earliest observations. |
| *c. 2200* | Tribal people from Iran destroyed Akkadian Empire. |
| | Middle Minoan age flourished on Crete because of control of Mediterranean. |
| | Beginning of Xia dynasty in China. |
| | Beginning of Middle Kingdom in Egypt. |
| *c. 2000* | Bronze Age began in Europe. |
| | Mesopotamian mathematicians solved quadratic equations. |
| | In astronomy, Babylonian priests made their first observational records. |
| *1925* | Hittites conquered Babylon. |
| *c. 1792* | Hammurabi became king of Babylonia and enacted a harsh legal code. |
| *c. 1730* | Invading Asian Hyksos people established their kingdom in the Nile Delta. |
| *c. 1650* | Hittite Old Kingdom established in Asia Minor. |
| *c. 1600* | Mycenean civilization spread into Greece. |
| *c. 1580* | Hyksos driven out of Egypt; beginning of New Kingdom. |
| *c. 1500* | Aryan invasion of India. |
| | Collapse of Indus Valley civilization. |

|  | Beginning of Shang dynasty in China. |
|---|---|
| *c. 1400* | Iron Age under way in India and W Asia. |
|  | Hittite New Empire established. |
|  | Egyptian empire at its peak under Amenhotep III. |
|  | Temple at Luxor, Upper Egypt, built. |
|  | Earthquake or war destroyed Minoan civilization. |
| *c. 1350* | Death of Tutankhamen, king of Egypt. |
| *c. 1321* | Temple of Abu Simbel built for Ramses II in Egypt. |
| *c. 1300* | First Celts appeared, in Upper Danube region. |
| *c. 1250* | Israelites under Moses left Egypt. |
|  | Sack of Troy by Greeks after ten-year Trojan War. |
| *c. 1200* | Phoenicians began to build up empire. |
|  | Chavín culture blossomed in Peru (to 300). |
| *c. 1100* | First Chinese dictionary published. |
|  | Rise of the Greek city-states began. |
| *1090* | Late New Kingdom began in Egypt: decline and division. |
| *c. 1066* | Zhou dynasty established in China. |
| *1025* | Hebrew monarchy founded. |
| *c. 1000–500* | Zapotecs in Mexico built ceremonial centre Monte Albn. |
| *c. 970* | Death of Hebrew king David; reign of King Solomon began. |
| *c. 937* | Hebrew kingdom divided into Israel and Judah. |
| *c. 900* | Etruscans settled in Italy. |

| | |
|---|---|
| *876* | A symbol for zero was used for the first time, in India. |
| *850* | Phoenicians founded Carthage. |
| *776* | First Olympic Games, in Greece. |
| *753* | Traditional date for founding of Rome. |
| *c. 733* | Assyrians destroyed Damascus. |
| *689* | Assyrians destroyed Babylon. |
| *663* | Egypt united under Psammetichus I. |
| *612* | Medes conquered Assyria and destroyed the capital, Nineveh. |
| *c. 604* | Lao Zi, founder of Taoism, born in China. |
| *c. 600* | Choral performances (dithyrambs) in honour of Dionysus formed the beginnings of Greek tragedy, according to Aristotle. |
| *586* | First diaspora of the Jews began when Babylonia under Nebuchadnezzar conquered Palestine. |
| | In Babylon, he constructed the hanging gardens. |
| *c. 563* | Gautama Siddhartha (later Buddha, the Enlightened One) born in Nepal. |

*The life of a creature passes like the torrent in the mountain and the lightning in the sky.*
**Buddha** attributed

| | |
|---|---|
| *551* | Philosopher Confucius (K'ung Tzu) born in China. |

*Study the past if you would divine the future.*
**Confucius**

| | |
|---|---|
| *550* | Cyrus the Great seized Median throne and began to build Persian empire. |
| | Greek mathematician Pythagoras formulated his theorem relating the lengths of the sides of a right-angled triangle. |
| | Aesop's *Fables* written in Greece. |
| *546* | Pythagoras developed the musical octave. |
| *539* | Cyrus annexed Asia Minor, Babylonia, Syria, and Palestine. |
| *539–529* | Jews allowed to return to Jerusalem. |
| *530* | Buddha preached his first sermon in Benares. |
| *525* | Persians conquered Egypt. |
| *510* | Roman republic founded. |
| *c. 500* | Beginning of Maya civilization in Yucatán. |
| | Magadha kingdom established in NW India. Vedda conquered by Sinhalese in Sri Lanka. |
| | First studies of the structure and behaviour of animals, by the Greek Alcmaeon of Creton. |
| | Beginning of the great age of Greek drama, which included tragedy, comedy, and satyr plays (grotesque farce). |
| *499* | Beginning of Greek-Persian wars. |
| *490* | Persian invading armies defeated by Greeks at Marathon. |
| *486* | First section of the Grand Canal of China built. |

---

*My tongue swore, but my mind's unsworn.*
**Euripides**
*Hippolytus* 429 BC

| | |
|---|---|
| *c. 484* | Birth of Greek dramatist Euripides, whose plays dealt with the emotions and reactions of ordinary people, rather than deities. |
| *480* | Battle of Thermopylae, in which 400 Spartans died trying to prevent Persian invasion of Greece. |
| | Greek navy destroyed Persian fleet at Salamis. |
| *468* | Sophocles' first victory at the Athens festival. His use of a third actor altered the course of the tragic form. |

---

*I depict men as they ought to be, but Euripides depicts them as they are.*
**Sophocles**

---

| | |
|---|---|
| *460* | Birth of Greek physician Hippocrates of Cos. *The Hippocratic Oath* is named after him. |

---

*The life so short, the craft so long to learn.*
**Hippocrates**
*Aphorisms*

---

| | |
|---|---|
| *458* | Aeschylus' three Oresteia plays were first performed. |
| | Greek philosopher Empedocles proposed that all substances are made up of a combination of four elements earth, air, fire, and water, an idea that was developed by Plato and Aristotle, and persisted for over 2,000 years. |
| | Hipparcos of Metapontum discovered that some numbers are irrational (cannot be expressed as |

|              | the ratio of two integers). |
| *447–438*    | Parthenon temple erected in Athens. |
| *431–40*     | Peloponnesian wars between Athens and Sparta; Athens defeated. |
| *429*        | Birth of Athenian philosopher Plato. |
| *c. 425*     | Aristophanes began writing comedies, which came to include *The Birds* 414, *Lysistrata* 411, and *The Frogs* 405. |
|              | In Greek tragedy the importance of the chorus diminished under Euripides, author of *The Bacchae* 405. |
| *405*        | Egypt once more independent. |
| *403*        | Warring states' period began in China. |
| *c. 400*     | Greek philosopher Democritus theorized that matter consists ultimately of tiny, indivisible particles, atomos. |

---

*The first principles of the universe are atoms and empty space; everything else is merely thought to exist.*
**Democritus**

---

| *399*        | Socrates condemned to death after accusations that his philosophical teachings were opposed to established ideas. |

---

*The unexamined life is not worth living.*
**Socrates**

---

| *390*        | Rome sacked by Gauls. |

| | |
|---|---|
| *378–371* | Sparta overthrown by Thebes. |
| *365* | Chinese observed the satellites of Jupiter with the naked eye. |
| *359* | Philip of Macedon became king of Macedonia. |
| *c. 350* | Menander's new comedy of social manners developed. |
| | Aristotle laid down the basic philosophy of the biological sciences and outlined a theory of evolution. |
| *338* | Philip of Macedon invaded Greece. |
| | The use of coins began in Rome. |
| *332* | Macedonians under Alexander the Great conquered Asia Minor, Phoenicia, Persia, and Egypt. |
| | Alexander founded the port of Alexandria. |
| *331* | Alexander destroyed the Persian empire. |
| *326* | Alexander stretched his empire as far as the river Indus. |
| *321* | Foundation of Mauryan dynasty, which was to unite most of India. |
| *313* | Tibet founded. |
| *312* | Work began on the Roman road, the Appian Way, from Rome to Brindisi. |
| *311* | Rome developed the world's first permanent navy. |
| *c. 300* | Rise of Maya civilization in Central America. |
| | Olmec of Central America disappeared, replaced by regional cultures. |
| | Agriculture began in Japan with the Yayoi period. |

Theophrastus carried out the first detailed studies of plants.

Euclid laid out the laws of geometry in his book *Elements*.

Hindu epic *Mahabharata* probably composed.

First six books of the Bible assembled.

Work began on the Colossus of Rhodes.

Great observatory built at Alexandria by Ptolemy.

**3rd century**   Aristarchus argued that the Sun is the centre of the Solar System.

Celts settled in the British Isles.

**287**   Greek mathematician Archimedes was born.

**279**   Lighthouse at Pharos, Alexandria one of the Seven Wonders completed.

**264–241**   First Punic War (Rome and Carthage), ending in Roman annexation of Sicily.

---

*The Romans boldly aspired to universal dominion and, what is more, achieved what they aimed at.*
  **Polybius** On the Punic Wars
*Histories II 38*

---

**c. 250**   Archimedes' principle of buoyancy was established.

**c. 240**   Emergence of Roman drama, adapted from Greek originals.

Plautus, Terence, and Seneca became the main playwrights.

| | |
|---|---|
| *c. 230* | Eratosthenes developed a method for finding all prime numbers. |
| *221* | Qin dynasty began in China. |
| *218*–201 | Second Punic War. |
| *216* | Hannibal of Carthage crossed the Alps to invade Italy. |
| *214* | Building of the Great Wall of China began, to keep out invaders. |
| *206* | Han dynasty began in China. |
| *c. 200* | Romans began to conquer Spain. |
| *c. 190* | Chinese mathematicians used powers of 10 to express magnitudes. |
| *155* | Indio-Greek kingdom in Indus Valley, founded by Menander. |
| *149–146* | Third Punic War: Carthage destroyed by Romans; Greece annexed by Rome. |
| *133* | Asia Minor became a province of Rome. |
| *108* | China annexed Korea. |
| *c. 100* | Chinese mathematicians began using negative numbers. |
| *98* | Trajan became Roman emperor, with empire at its largest. |
| *70* | Roman poet Virgil was born. |
| *66–62* | Romans conquered Syria and Palestine. |
| *60* | First Triumvirate formed in Rome. |
| *55* | Roman invasion of Britain began; Julius Caesar made reconnaissance. |
| *54* | Julius Caesar's second expedition into Britain he took his army across the Thames and the defence disintegrated. |

| | |
|---|---|
| *51* | Romans completed conquest of Gaul. |
| *45* | The Julian calendar as used in most Western countries was introduced. |
| *44* | Julius Caesar assassinated. |
| *43* | Second Triumvirate formed. |
| | Cleopatra became queen of Egypt. |
| *31* | Battle of Actium, where the combined fleets of Mark Antony and Cleopatra were defeated by a Roman fleet under Augustus. |
| *30* | Egypt became a province of Rome. |
| | Virgil began writing the *Aeneid*. |

---

*We may be masters of our every lot/By bearing it.*
**Virgil**
*Aeneid*

---

| | |
|---|---|
| *27* | Augustus proclaimed the first Roman emperor. |
| | The building of the Pantheon in Rome began. |
| *4* | Birth of Jesus Christ in Bethlehem. |
| *1st century* | Chinese invented the rudder. |

# AD

| | |
|---|---|
| *1* | Gold, silver, copper, lead, iron, tin, and mercury were known. |
| *14* | Augustus Caesar died and was succeeded by Tiberius as emperor of Rome. |
| *27* | Jesus Christ baptized. |
| *28* | John the Baptist executed. |
| *30* | Jesus Christ crucified. |
| *32* | Saul of Tarsus converted to Christianity and was baptized as Paul; later canonized as St Paul. |
| *37* | Tiberius died and was succeeded by Caligula. |
| *42* | Caligula assassinated; succeeded by Claudius. |
| *43* | Romans under Aulus Plautius invaded Britain. |
| *c. 50* | Rise of kingdom of Aksum in NE Africa. |
| *54* | Claudius murdered; Nero became emperor of Rome. |
| *57* | First Japanese envoys to China. |
| *60* | Queen Boudicca revolted against Romans in Britain. |
| *64* | Great fire of Rome; emperor Nero blamed Christians. |
| *70* | Revolt of Jews against Rome. |
| | Jerusalem sacked by the Romans under Titus. |
| *78* | Pliny the Elder published books I-X of *Historia Naturalis*. |
| *79* | Pompeii and Herculaneum destroyed by volcanic eruption of Mount Vesuvius. |
| *84* | The building of the Roman baths at Bath, England, was begun. |

| | |
|---|---|
| *91* | Han people invaded Mongolia. |
| *105* | Paper was made in China. |
| *106* | Jordan became part of Roman province of Arabia. |
| *115* | The Roman Empire reached its greatest extent. |
| *122* | Hadrian's Wall built in Britain. |
| *c. 150* | Ptolemy promulgated his complicated Earth-centred system, which dominated the astronomy of the Middle Ages. |
| *161* | The Acropolis was built in Athens. |
| *c. 175* | Greek physician Galen established the basic principles of anatomy and physiology. |
| *c. 200* | Huns invaded Afghanistan, ruling to 540. |
| | Arawak Indians began migration from NE South America to Caribbean. |
| | The Arabs and Romans developed fore-and-aft rigging that allowed boats to sail across the direction of wind. |
| | In chemistry, the techniques of solution, filtration, and distillation were known. |
| *220* | Three Kingdoms period began in China. |
| | Goths invaded Asia Minor and Balkan Peninsula. |
| *225* | Romans completed conquest of Cisalpine Gaul. |
| *226* | Foundation of Sassanian Empire in Persia. |
| *c. 250* | Diophantus of Alexandria wrote the first book on algebra. |
| *268* | Goths sacked Athens, Sparta, and Corinth. |
| *4th century* | Yamato state, core of Japan, established. |
| *313* | Edict of Milan; Emperor Constantine established |

|  |  |
|---|---|
|  | Christianity as the religion of the Roman Empire. |
| *320* | Beginning of the Gupta Empire in India. |
| *330* | Constantine the Great shifted seat of power to Byzantium, renamed Constantinople, and briefly united Roman Empire. |
| *342* | Goths destroyed the protectorate of Bosporus. |
| *360* | Huns invaded Europe. |
| *367* | The Romans in Britain defeated by Picts, Scots, and Saxons. |
| *c. 375* | Kálidása's *Sakuntalá* marked the height of Sanskrit drama in India. |
| *376* | Huns invaded Russia. |
| *395* | Roman Empire split into Western and Eastern (Byzantine) empires. |
| *c. 400* | Beginning of a hundred years of invasions by Picts, Saxons, Jutes, and Angles into Britain. |
|  | Beginning of Mon kingdom in Burma. |
| *401–10* | Roman legions withdrew from Britain. |
| *409* | Visigoths established a kingdom in Spain. |
| *410* | Visigoths under Alaric sacked Rome. |
| *425* | Barbarians (outsiders) settled in Roman provinces. |
| *432* | St Patrick, according to tradition, brought Christianity to Ireland. |
| *433* | Attila became ruler of the Huns. |
| *439* | Vandals captured Carthage. |
| *451–52* | Attila the Hun invaded Gaul, ultimately unsuccessful. |
| *452* | The city of Venice was founded. |

|         |                                                                                        |
|---------|----------------------------------------------------------------------------------------|
|         | The city of Milan was destroyed by Attila the Hun.                                      |
| *455*   | Rome sacked by Vandals.                                                                 |
| *470*   | Huns withdrew from Europe.                                                              |
| *476*   | Fall of the (Western) Roman Empire.                                                     |
| *481*   | Clovis became king of the Franks.                                                       |
| *488–93*| Ostrogoths conquered Italy.                                                             |
| *496*   | Franks conquered the Alemanni (German peoples).                                         |
| *c. 500*| Huns secured control over NW India.                                                     |
|         | Native Americans in Mississippi basin became farmers with small settlements.           |
| *507*   | Franks expelled Visigoths from France.                                                  |
| *c. 508*| Clovis made Paris his capital.                                                          |
| *525*   | Abyssinians conquered Yemen.                                                            |
| *534*   | Byzantines reconquered N Africa.                                                        |
| *535–55*| Byzantines reconquered Italy.                                                           |
| *539*   | War between Byzantines and Persia.                                                      |
|         | Milan sacked by Goths.                                                                  |
| *542–543*| Widespread epidemic of the plague.                                                    |
| *550*   | End of Gupta Empire in India.                                                           |
|         | Toltec kingdom continued Teotihuacan civilization.                                      |
| *552*   | Buddhism introduced to Japan.                                                           |
| *563*   | St Columba arrived on Iona in the Western Isles of Scotland and began his conversion of the Picts to Christianity. |
|         | He founded a monastery there.                                                           |
| *570*   | Muhammad, founder of Islam, born in Mecca.                                              |

*And do not say regarding anything, I am going to do that tomorrow, but only if God will.*
**The Koran**

| | |
|---|---|
| *572* | War between Byzantine Empire and Persia. |
| *575* | Persians overthrew Abyssinians in Yemen. |
| *581* | Sui dynasty united China. |
| *590* | St Gregory the Great was elected pope. |
| | His enlightened leadership inspired church music to new heights, initiating Gregorian chant. |
| *597* | St Augustine brought the Benedictine order to England and founded a monastery at Canterbury. |
| *600* | Beginning of the Harsha dynasty in India. |
| | A decimal number system was developed in India. |
| *604* | Shōtoku Taishi, regent of Japan, promulgated 17 principles of government. |
| *610* | First revelation of Muhammad. |
| *616* | Egypt invaded by Persians. |
| | Khmer Empire founded in SE Asia. |
| *618* | Persians conquered Egypt. |
| | Beginning of Tang dynasty in China. |
| *622* | Flight of Muhammad from Mecca to Medina: start of Islamic calendar. |
| *632* | Death of Muhammad. |
| *633* | Arabs conquered Persia. |
| *637* | Sassanian Empire destroyed by Muslims. |
| *638* | Burma founded. |
| *641* | Arabs conquered Egypt. |

| | |
|---|---|
| *644* | China invaded Korea. |
| *646* | Taika reform in Japan nationalized land and introduced Chinese-style bureaucracy. |
| *650* | Byzantine Empire partly overrun by Muslims. |
| *661* | Omayyad dynasty of the Islamic Empire founded. |
| *664* | Synod of Whitby decided to adopt Roman, not Celtic, form of Christianity for Britain. |
| *685* | Picts stopped Northumbrians invading Scotland. |
| *697* | Arabs destroyed Carthage. |
| *c. 700* | Hinduism began to drive Buddhism from India. |
| | The Anglo-Saxon poem *Beowulf* composed. |
| *710* | Nara became capital of Japan (until 784). |
| *711* | Moors invaded Spain. |
| *712* | Muslims conquered Sind (now a province of Pakistan). |
| *720* | Moors invaded France. |
| *731* | The Venerable Bede wrote *Ecclesiastical History of the English People*. |
| *732* | Moors driven out of France by Charles Martel. |
| *740* | Gurjara dynasty united N India and defeated the Arabs. |
| *750* | Abbasid caliphate founded in Baghdad. |
| | St Boniface took Christianity from England into Germany. |
| *751* | Pepin the Short deposed the last Merovingian king of the Franks and founded the Carolingian dynasty. |
| *760* | Turkish Empire founded. |
| | Baghdad founded. |

| | |
|---|---|
| *771* | Charlemagne conquered Saxony and continued campaign for Carolingians. |
| *782* | Offa's Dyke, an earthwork between the rivers Wye and Dee, built to prevent attacks into England by Welsh tribes. |
| *793* | Square-rigged Viking longboats began to cross the N Sea to raid the British Isles. |
| *794* | Beginning of the Heian period in Japan (to 1185) with the capital at Kyoto, which saw a great flourishing of art and literature. |
| *c. 800* | Rajputs began to set up kingdom in India. |
| | City of Machu Pichu, Peru, developed. |
| *800* | Charlemagne crowned Holy Roman emperor by pope on 25 Dec. |
| *809* | Death of Haroun-al-Raschid began 200 years of chaos in Arab Empire. |
| *811* | Bulgars defeated Byzantines. |
| *826* | Arabs conquered Crete. |
| *829* | Persian mathematician Muhammad ibn-Musa al-Khwarizmi published a work on algebra that made use of the decimal number system. |
| *832* | Sicily captured by Saracens. |
| *840* | Dublin founded by Danes. |
| *844* | Scotland unified under Kenneth MacAlpin. |
| *845* | Buddhism proscribed in China. |
| *846* | Rome sacked by Arabs. |
| *850* | The acropolis of Zimbabwe built in South Africa. |
| | The astrolabe (a navigation instrument) perfected by Arabs. |

|        |                                                                      |
|--------|----------------------------------------------------------------------|
|        | Frankish (Carolingian) Empire broken up.                             |
| *862*  | Novgorod founded by Vikings.                                         |
| *867*  | Basil I began Macedonian dynasty of Byzantine Empire (to 1056).      |
| *869*  | Malta captured by Arabs.                                             |
| *871*  | Accession of Alfred the Great as king of Wessex.                    |
| *874*  | Vikings settled in Iceland.                                          |
| *878*  | Treaty of Wedmore between King Alfred and the Danes.                |
| *882*  | Kiev replaced Novgorod as capital of Russia.                        |
| *885*  | Viking siege of Paris.                                              |
| *891*  | Anglo-Saxon Chronicle begun.                                        |
| *900*  | Start of Christian re-conquest of Spain.                           |
| *c. 907* | Chola power established in S India.                                |
|        | Commercial treaties between Kiev and Constantinople.               |
|        | Civil war and the Five Dynasties and Ten Kingdoms period began in China. |
| *909*  | Fatimid dynasty founded in N Africa.                               |
| *912*  | The French province of Normandy was granted as a duchy to Viking leader Rollo and his Norsemen. |
| *915*  | Fatimid armies invaded Egypt.                                       |
| *918*  | Fatimid armies invaded Egypt again.                                |
| *919*  | Henry the Fowler became Henry I of Germany.                        |
| *925*  | End of classical Maya period in Yucatán.                           |
| *930*  | Iceland's parliament first convened.                               |
| *935*  | Fatimid armies defeated in Egypt.                                  |

| | |
|---|---|
| *936* | Otto succeeded his father Henry I as king of Germany. |
| *959* | Edgar crowned king of all England. |
| *960* | Song dynasty began in China. |
| *961* | Byzantine armies took back Crete from Arabs. |
| *962* | Otto I of Germany crowned Holy Roman emperor. |
| *965* | Byzantine armies took back Cyprus from Arabs. |
| *969* | Fatimids conquered Egypt. |
| *985* | Toltecs now controlled Mexico. |
| | Viking settlements in Greenland. |
| *987* | Capetian dynasty founded in France. |
| | League of Mayapán founded in South America. |
| *991* | Renewed Viking raids on England. |
| *994* | London besieged by Danes and Norsemen. |
| *c. 1000* | Rise of Kanem Empire (N Nigeria). |
| | Chim state formed in Peru. |
| | Caribs from South America destroyed Arawak culture in Caribbean. |
| | Viking Leif Ericsson said to have reached Nova Scotia. |
| | *The Tale of Genji*, possibly the world's first psychological novel, written by a lady at the Japanese court. |
| | .Chinese perfected gunpowder. |
| *1016* | Danish invader Canute gained throne of England. |
| *1018* | Byzantines conquered Bulgarians. |
| *1023* | Abbadid Muslim dynasty in Seville. |

| | |
|---|---|
| *1028* | Canute accepted as king of Norway after invasion. |
| *1035* | Moors evicted from Aragon, which became a Spanish kingdom. |
| *1040* | Duncan, king of the Scots, murdered by Macbeth, who proclaimed himself king. |
| *1042* | Edward the Confessor became king of England. |
| *1045* | Byzantines conquered Armenia. |
| | Milan became an independent city-state. |
| *c. 1050* | Almoravid empire in Morocco began. |
| | Start of main Muslim invasions into India from Afghanistan. |
| | *Rubaiyat*, a collection of poems, written by Omar Khayyam. |
| | Collapse of Hindu kingdoms. |
| *1054* | Schism between Roman and Greek Orthodox churches. |
| | Abdallah ben Yasim began Muslim conquest of W Africa. |
| *1055* | Seljuk Turks took over caliphate. |
| *1057* | Macbeth murdered by Malcolm. |
| *1061* | Almoravids conquered N Africa. |
| | Normans conquered Messina. |
| *1065* | Westminster Abbey in London consecrated under Edward the Confessor. |
| *1066* | Battle of Hastings, 14 Oct: Normans under William the Conqueror defeated Harold II and conquered England. |
| *1067* | The Bayeux Tapestry was begun. |
| *1071* | Turks conquered Minor Asia. |

| | |
|---|---|
| *1075* | Conflict between papacy and Holy Roman Empire began. |
| *1084* | Normans sacked Rome. |
| *1085* | Civil war in Ireland. |
| *1086* | Domesday Book of England completed. |
| *1087* | William I of England fatally wounded at the Battle of Nantes; he was succeeded by his son William II. |
| *1090* | The Chinese invented the magnetic compass. |
| *1093* | Norman-style Durham Cathedral begun in NE England. |
| *1095–99* | First Crusade. |
| *1100* | William II of England killed while hunting in the New Forest; his brother Henry became king. |
| *1109* | War began between England and France. |
| | Nahuas in control of central Mexican plateau. |
| | Alcohol was first distilled. |
| *1113* | Order of Knights Hospitallers of St John of Jerusalem founded. |
| *1119* | Military Christian order of Knights Templars founded. |
| *1122* | Concordat of Worms brought compromise between emperor and pope. |
| *1127* | Normans completed conquest of Sicily. |
| | City-state of Muscovy (Moscow) founded. |
| | Southern Song dynasty settled in China. |
| *1144* | Republican rule established in Rome. |
| *1147* | Portugal became independent monarchy. |
| *1147–49* | Second Crusade. |
| *1148* | Crusaders defeated at Damascus. |

| | |
|---|---|
| *1150* | Mechanical clocks first appeared in Europe. |
| *1152* | Frederick Barbarossa became king of the Germans. |
| *1154* | Plantagenet succession began in England when Henry of Anjou acceded to the throne. |
| *1157* | Thomas Becket became chancellor of England. |
| *1160* | Normans expelled from N Africa. |
| *1162* | Thomas Becket appointed archbishop of Canterbury. |
| *1163* | The construction of Notre Dame in Paris was begun. |
| *1164–74* | Saladin conquered Egypt. |
| *1167* | Oxford University founded. |
| | Anglo-Norman adventurers invaded Ireland. |
| *1168* | Toltec capital Tula fell to the Aztecs. |
| *1169* | English invaded Ireland. |
| | Serbian kingdom united. |
| *1170* | Thomas à Becket murdered. |
| *1174* | Saladin launched holy war against Christians. |
| *1175* | Egypt split into two kingdoms. |
| *1176* | Turks defeated Byzantium over Asia Minor in Battle of Myriokephalon. |
| *1180* | Toltec state fell to nomadic tribes. |
| *1185* | Defeat of the Taira (Heike) by the rival Minamoto (Genji) clan at naval battle of Dannoura, Japan, ended the Gempei War (began 1180). |
| *1187* | Saladin defeated Christians at Hittin and went on to take Jerusalem. |
| *1189* | Richard I became king of England. |

| | |
|---|---|
| *1189–92* | Third Crusade, led by Richard, Philip II of France, and Frederick I (Barbarossa). |
| *1192* | Kamakura shogunate began in Japan (to 1333). |
| | Richard I made truce with Saladin but was captured by Leopold of Austria while returning to England. |
| *1194* | Chichén Itzá, Toltec city in Yucatán, fell. |
| | Chartres Cathedral was begun in France. |
| *1198* | Florence became an independent republic. |
| *1199* | Richard I killed during war with France: John succeeded him to the throne of England. |
| *1200* | Foundation of Aztec Empire in N Mexico. |
| | Christian Sudan kingdoms invaded by Muslims. |
| *1202* | Italian mathematician Leonardo Fibonacci studied the sequence of numbers (1, 1, 2, 3, 5, 8, 13, 21, ...) in which each number is the sum of the two preceding ones; published in Liber Abaci. |
| *1202–04* | Fourth Crusade. |
| *1204* | Crusaders sacked Constantinople. |
| | King John of England lost Normandy to France. |
| *1206* | Genghis Khan became ruler of all Mongol peoples in E Asia. |
| | Delhi sultanate founded, the first Muslim dynasty in India. |
| *1212* | War broke out again between England and France. |
| | Thousands of children embarked on the ill-fated Children's Crusade. |
| *1213* | Mongols, led by Genghis Khan, invaded China. |

| | |
|---|---|
| *1214* | Beijing captured by Mongol forces. |
| *1215* | King John of England forced to seal Magna Carta, granting rights to nobles, on 15 June. |

---

*To no man will we sell, or deny, or delay, right or justice.*
**Magna Carta** 1215

---

| | |
|---|---|
| *1216* | King John died; succeeded by child Henry III. |
| *1218–21* | Fifth Crusade captured and then lost Damietta, Egypt. |
| *1219* | Mongols defeated Samarkand, Bokhara, and Persia. |
| *1220* | Work began on the building of Salisbury Cathedral. |
| *1221* | Mongols attacked Delhi sultanate. |
| *1223* | Mongols overran steppes of Russia. |
| *1224* | War broke out again between England and France. |
| *1227* | Henry III came of age. |
| | Genghis Khan died; empire divided among his three sons. |
| *1228* | Francis of Assisi canonized two years after his death. |
| *1229* | Frederick II, Holy Roman emperor, crowned king of Jerusalem as a result of Sixth Crusade (1228–29), with no fighting. |
| *1230* | Crusaders brought leprosy to Europe. |
| | Teutonic Knights (Christian military order) gained control of Latvia. |

| | |
|---|---|
| *1236* | Arabs lost Cordoba to Ferdinand III of Castile. |
| *1237* | Mongols invaded Russia for the second time; the Golden Horde began to terrorize Europe. |
| *1240* | Mongols took Moscow and Kiev. |
| | Mali Empire founded in W Africa. |
| *1241* | Mongols defeated Germans and invaded Poland and Hungary, but later withdrew from Europe. |
| *1242* | Gunpowder introduced to Europe from the Far East. |
| | War broke out between England and France. |
| *1243* | End of Seljuk dynasty of Turks. |
| *1245* | Frederick II de-throned by Council of Lyons as part of long-running feud with pope. |
| *1248* | Cologne Cathedral begun. |
| *1249* | Roger Bacon noted the existence of explosives. |
| *1250* | Inca settled at Cuzco, S Peru. |
| | Chimú established in N Peru. |
| | Mameluke dynasty in Egypt began. |
| | Saracens captured Louis IX. |
| | Unidentified epidemic weakened native American civilization. |
| *1252* | The Inquisition (Roman Catholic agency for suppressing heresy) began to use torture. |
| *1258* | Mongols took Baghdad. |
| *1259* | Treaty of Paris (France and England). |
| | Kublai Khan became Mongol emperor of China. |
| | Mongols invaded Syria. |
| *1261–63* | Vikings on Iceland and Greenland accepted Norwegian sovereignty. |

| | |
|---|---|
| *1264* | Thomas Aquinas completed *Summa contra Gentiles/Against the Errors of the Infidels*, a treatise on reason and faith. |
| *1264–67* | Second Barons' War in England between Henry III and nobles under Simon de Montfort. |
| *1265* | Birth of English Parliament when Simon de Montfort summoned representatives of the boroughs as well as the shires. |
| | Italian poet Dante Alighieri was born. |
| *1266* | Roger Bacon in England began his *Opus Majus/ Great Work*, a compendium of all branches of knowledge. |
| *1271–75* | Marco Polo travelled overland from Venice to China. |

---

*I have not told half of what I saw.*
**Marco Polo**
Last words

---

| | |
|---|---|
| *1272* | Henry III of England died and was succeeded by Edward I. |
| *1274* | Mongol army sent to invade Japan was repelled with aid of storm perceived as 'divine wind' (kamikaze). |
| | Thomas Aquinas died. |
| *1275* | Marco Polo began to serve Kublai Khan. |
| *1279* | Mongols in control over whole of China. |
| | Yuan dynasty in China founded by Kublai Khan. |
| *1280* | *Carmina Burana*, a collection of students' songs, was compiled in Benediktbuern, Bavaria. |
| *1281* | Second Mongol invasion attempt on Japan also |

failed because of high winds.

| | |
|---|---|
| *1282* | Sicilians rose against Normans. |
| *1283* | Edward I began building Caernarvon Castle in N Wales. |
| *1284* | Kingdom of Navarre joined to France through marriage. |
| *1285* | Egyptians and Hittites fought over, then divided, Syria. |
| *1288* | France's greatest troubadour, Adam de la Halle, died in Naples. |
| | Spectacles were invented. |
| *1290* | England expelled Jews. |
| *1291* | Core of Switzerland formed by cantons of Schwyz, Uri, and Lower Unterwalden in league against Habsburg overlords. |
| | Acre, the last Christian fortress in Syria, was taken by Muslims. |
| *1294* | Start of Franco-Scottish alliance. |
| | Kublai Khan died. |
| *14th century* | The Renaissance began to revive interest in Classical Greek and Roman art and architecture, including ruins and buried art and artefacts. |
| *1300* | Ottoman Empire founded by Turkish sultan Osman I. |
| | Edward I invaded Scotland. |
| | Guns invented by Arabs. |
| *1306* | Robert Bruce became King Robert I of Scotland. |
| | Giotto completed his fresco cycle in the Arena Chapel in Padua. |
| *1307* | Edward I of England died; succeeded by |

Edward II.

Dante began writing *The Divine Comedy.*

---

*There is no greater sorrow than to recall a time of happiness in misery.*
**Dante**
*Divine Comedy: Inferno, V*

---

| | |
|---|---|
| *1313* | Cannon invented by German monk Berthold Schwarz (attributed). |
| *1314* | Battle of Bannockburn: Robert Bruce defeated English under Edward II. |
| | Completion of the *Mappa Mundi* symbolic map of the world with Jerusalem at its centre. |
| *1321* | Dante Alighieri died. |
| *1324* | Danes sold Estonia to Teutonic Knights. |
| *1325* | Sultanate of Delhi at its height under Muhammad ibn Tughluq. |
| | Aztecs in Mexico founded their capital city Tenochtitlán. |
| *1327* | Edward II deposed and murdered in Berkeley Castle; succeeded by Edward III. |
| *1329* | Robert Bruce died; David II acceded to throne of Scotland. |
| *1332* | English Parliament divided into two houses for the first time. |
| *1333* | Sienese painter Simone Martini created *Annunciation* altarpiece. |
| *1336* | Kingdom of Vijayanagar founded in S India. |
| | Rival northern and southern courts in Japan |

|  |  |
|---|---|
|  | (until 1392). |
| *1337* | Edward III claimed French crown. |
|  | Hundred Years' War began between England and France. |
| *1339* | Ashikaga shogunate established in Japan. |
| *1340* | Geoffrey Chaucer born in London. |
|  | French defeated by English in sea battle off Sluis. |
| *1341* | Petrarch (Francesco Petrarca) crowned poet laureate in the Capitol, Rome. |
| *1346* | Battle of Crécy, in which gunpowder was used probably for the first time in battle. |
|  | The French were defeated by the English. |
| *c. 1348* | Edward III founded Most Noble Order of the Garter. |
|  | Bubonic plague came to Europe from India or China; came to be called Black Death in 19th century. It was to kill more than one-third of the population of Europe in the next few years. |
|  | Giovanni Boccaccio's collection of tales *The Decameron* brought together. |
| *1350* | Siam founded. |
|  | Middle English poem *Sir Gawayne and the Greene Knight* written. |
|  | Firoz Shah became sultan of Delhi. |
| *1353* | Turks began invasion of Europe. |
| *1354* | Turks took Gallipoli. |
| *1355* | Illayas Shad established independent Bengal. |
| *1356* | English defeated French in Battle of Poitiers. |
|  | Ottoman Turks entered Europe. |

| | |
|---|---|
| *1357* | Turks captured Adrianople (now Edirne). |
| *1360* | Treaty of Brétigny ended first stage of Hundred Years' War. |
| *1362* | First version of William Langland's *Piers Plowman.* |

---

*In a somer season, when soft was the sonne.*
**William Langland**
*Piers Plowman* Prologue

---

| | |
|---|---|
| *1363* | Tamerlane began conquest of Asia. |
| *1364* | Music's first large-scale masterpiece, the *Notre Dame Mass of Guillaume de Machaut,* performed in Rheims at the coronation of Charles V of France. |
| *1368* | Mongols expelled from China. |
| | Ming dynasty began in China and made Nanjing their capital. |
| | Tamerlane ascended throne of Samarkand. |
| *1372* | English defeated by French, who took Poitiers, Angoulme, and La Rochelle. |
| *1375* | Nō (or Noh) drama began to develop in Japan. |
| *1377* | Edward III of England died; succeeded by Richard II. |
| | Malays established settlement of Malacca. |
| *1378* | Great Schism of Rome and Avignon began, with two rival popes. |
| | England at war again with France, Spain, and Scotland. |
| *1380* | Tamerlane began series of conquests, including |

Persia, Georgia, Russia, and Egypt.

| | |
|---|---|
| *1381* | Peasants' Revolt in England. |
| *1382* | First translation of the Bible into English, by John Wycliffe. |
| | Turks captured Sofia. |
| *1385* | Portugal ensured independence from Spain. |
| *1387* | Geoffrey Chaucer's *Canterbury Tales* collected. |

---

*He was a verray parfit gentil knyght.*
**Geoffrey Chaucer**
*The Canterbury Tales* Prologue

---

| | |
|---|---|
| *1389* | Serbian defeat at Kosovo brought them under Turkish domination. |
| *1395* | Tamerlane defeated the Golden Horde. |
| *1396* | Battle of Nicopolis: King Sigismund of Hungary's Christian army defeated by Ottoman sultan Bajazet. |
| | Last Bulgarian stronghold fell to the Turks, who controlled Bulgaria for next 500 years. |
| *1397* | Union of Kalmar united Sweden, Norway, and Denmark. |
| *1398* | Tamerlane invaded India, sacked Delhi, and annexed Punjab. |
| *1399* | Richard II of England deposed; Henry of Lancaster took throne as Henry IV. |
| *1400* | Richard II probably assassinated. |
| | Owen Glendower revolted in Wales |
| | Aztec Empire grew to cover most of Mexico. |
| | Hanseatic League at its height as trading |

confederation of more than 160 cities in N Europe.

| | |
|---|---|
| *1401* | Tamerlane conquered Damascus and Baghdad. |
| | Union of Poland and Lithuania. |
| *1402* | Henry IV invaded Wales. |
| | Tamerlane defeated Sultan Bajazet at Ankara and captured him. |
| *1403* | Ming dynasty began to extend territories in China. |
| *1405* | Tamerlane died while invading China; succeeded by Shah Rokh. |
| *1407* | Chinese ships reached Ceylon (Sri Lanka). |
| *1410* | Battle of Tannenberg in which Poles and Lithuanians defeated the Teutonic Knights. |
| *1412* | Joan of Arc born. |
| *1413* | Henry IV died; succeeded by Henry V. |
| *1415* | English defeated French at Battle of Agincourt. |
| *1416* | Venetians defeated Turks off Gallipoli. |
| *1417* | Great Schism ended by Council of Constance. |
| *1419* | Portuguese prince Henry the Navigator established a school for naval explorers. |
| *1421* | Beijing restored as capital of China. |
| *1422* | Henry V died in France; succeeded by his infant son Henry VI. |
| *1429* | Joan of Arc, leading French troops, raised English siege of Orléans. |
| *1430* | Chinese ships reached the Red Sea. |
| *1431* | Joan of Arc burned to death at the stake for witchcraft. |
| | Henry VI of England crowned king of France. |

*Everything I have done that was good I did by command of my voices.*
**Joan of Arc**
**During her trial** 1431

| | |
|---|---|
| *1432* | *The Adoration of the Mystical Lamb* altarpiece completed by Flemish painter Jan van Eyck. |
| *1434* | Medici dynasty came to power in Florence. |
| *1436* | *Della pittura* by Florentine Leon Battista Alberti laid the basis of art theory and mathematical perspective. |
| *1438* | Inca rebuilt Cuzco and began expansion. |
| | Filippo Brunelleschi completed the dome of Florence cathedral. |
| *1440* | Aztecs crowned Montezuma I. |
| | Battle of Cuzco: Inca defeated Chanca. |
| | Johann Gutenberg set up Europe's first printing business in Mainz, Germany. |
| | Public school Eton College founded in England. |
| *1441* | Maya new empire broken up into smaller states. |
| *1442* | First black slaves sent to Portugal. |
| *1447* | Break-up of Tamerlane's empire: India, Persia, and Afghanistan became independent. |
| *1448* | Portuguese built first European fort on African coast, at Arguin (Mauritania). |
| *1449* | Sweden broke away from Denmark and Norway. First known patent issued by Henry VI, for the stained glass for Eton College. |
| *1450* | Sforza dynasty supplanted the Viscontis in Milan. |

| | |
|---|---|
| *1451* | Mohammed II became emir of Turkey. |
| *1452* | Practice of slavery endorsed by pope. |
| *1453* | John Dunstable, England's first significant composer, died in London. |
| *1453* | End of Hundred Years' War. |
| | Turks with Mohammed II took Constantinople. |
| *1454* | Peace of Lodi between Venice and Milan. |
| *1455–85* | Wars of the Roses, civil wars in England between houses of Lancaster and York. |
| *1456* | Turks conquered Athens. |
| *1459* | Turks overran Serbia. |
| *1460* | Denmark annexed the duchies of Schleswig and Holstein from the Holy Roman Empire. |
| *1461* | Edward of York crowned king of England. |
| *1462* | Castile captured Gibraltar from Arabs. |
| *1463* | Turks conquered Bosnia. |
| | Turks at war with Venice. |
| *1467–77* | Onin war in Japan began a century of sporadic civil war; Kyoto burned. |
| *1468* | Songhai Empire began to grow in NW Africa. |
| *1470* | Portuguese reached Gold Coast of W Africa. |
| | Thomas Malory translated and modified *Le Morte D'Arthur*. |
| *1471* | William Caxton, working in Belgium, printed first book in English. |
| | Henry VI murdered in Tower of London. |
| | Portuguese sailors reached the Gulf of Guinea. |
| | Edward of York became King Edward IV for the second time. |

German artist Albrecht Dürer born in Nuremberg.

*1473*   The earliest known printed music, the *Collectorium super Magnificat* by Johannes Gerson, was published in Esslingen, near Stuttgart.

Polish astronomer Nicolaus Copernicus born.

*1475*   Turkey took over Crimea.

*1476*   Inca conquered Chimú (Ecuador).

*1477*   William Caxton produced the first book printed in England, *Dictes or Sayengis of the Philosophres*.

*1479*   Peace of Constantinople: Venice ceded territory in Albania and Lemnos to Turks.

Aragon and Castile united under Ferdinand and Isabella as kingdom of Spain.

Navarre divided between Spain and France. Treaty of Alvaovas between Spain and Portugal about Atlantic islands.

*1480*   Ivan III of Moscow overthrew Mongols.

Inca took over Bolivia.

Leonardo da Vinci designed small parachutes.

*1482*   Portuguese set up trading base on Gold Coast (Ghana).

*1483*   Edward IV of England died; his son Edward V was deposed and is believed to have been murdered.

Richard of Gloucester was made king as Richard III.

Burgundy and Brittany annexed by France.

Russians began to explore Siberia.

| | |
|---|---|
| *1484* | Inca conquered N and central Chile and NW Argentina. |
| | Portuguese reached mouth of river Congo in W Africa. |
| | Painter Sandro Botticelli in Florence completed *Birth of Venus.* |
| *1485* | Battle of Bosworth; Richard III defeated and killed by Henry Tudor, who acceded to the throne as Henry VII. |
| | English military corps Yeomen of the Guard established. |
| *1486* | Portuguese sailors reached Angola. |
| *1487* | Star Chamber court established in England by Henry VII. |
| *1488* | Portuguese explorer Bartolomeu Diaz became the first European to sail round Cape of Good Hope (then known as Cape of Storms) and establish route around Africa. |
| *1489* | Treaty of Dordrecht: alliance between Henry VII and Holy Roman emperor Frederick III. |
| *c. 1489* | City of Bijapur in Karnataka, India, founded as capital of the Muslim kingdom of Biafra. |
| *1492* | Italian navigator Christopher Columbus first sighted land in the W Indies on 12 Oct. |

*I must sail on until with the help of our Lord I discover land.*
**Christopher Columbus**
To crew the day before sighting America 1492 (traditional)

Spain took Granada from Muslims.

Leonardo da Vinci designed a flying machine.

Italian painter Piero della Francesca died.

**1494**   Treaty of Tordesillas between Spain and Portugal sharing the territories of the New World.

Summa de Arithmetica, a textbook of arithmetic and algebra, published in Venice by Luca Pacioli.

**c. 1495**   Everyman, the best known of all the morality plays, was first performed.

Charles VIII of France entered Naples; forced to leave by Holy League.

Diet (assembly) of Worms imposed Common Penny tax throughout the Holy Roman Empire.

**1496**   Aztecs captured Tehuantepec.

Bartolomeo Columbus (brother of Christopher) founded Santo Domingo, the first colonial city in the Americas.

Naval dockyard established at Portsmouth, S England.

**1497**   Perkin Warbeck, a Fleming claiming to be Richard, brother of Edward V, led unsuccessful rising against Henry VII.

Giovanni Caboto, on voyage of discovery for England, landed at Newfoundland.

Spanish settled island of Hispaniola.

Leonardo da Vinci painted The Last Supper in Milan.

**1498**   Vasco da Gama of Portugal reached India, having discovered a sea route from Europe to the subcontinent.

Caboto touched the coast of Greenland.

Columbus reached mainland South America.

**1499**      Safavi dynasty established in Persia.

**c. 1500**   Olmec civilization in Central America.

Farming settlements developed in Peru.

Italian commedia dell'arte troupes performed popular, improvised comedies.

Leonardo da Vinci studied human anatomy to improve his drawing ability and produced detailed anatomical drawings.

---

*The poet ranks far below the painter in the representation of visible things–and far below the musician in that of invisible things.*
**Leonardo da Vinci**
Selection from the Notebooks

---

Tramways – wooden tracks along which trolleys ran – were in use in mines.

**1500**      Portuguese explorer Pedro Cabral, on his way to the East Indies, accidentally reached coast of Brazil.

City of Basel joined the Swiss confederation.

**1502**      Portuguese settlement founded in Mozambique.

Montezuma II became Aztec emperor.

**1502–04**   Columbus, on his last voyage, explored Gulf of Mexico and Nicaragua.

**1503**      Leonardo da Vinci began painting the *Mona Lisa*.

| | |
|---|---|
| **1504** | Treaty of Lyons: France ceded Naples to Spain. |
| | Michelangelo's sculpture *David* completed. |
| **1505** | Trading contracts between India and Portugal. |
| | Mozambique became a Portuguese colony. |
| | Spanish conquered Puerto Rico. |
| **1506** | Work began on rebuilding St Peter's Cathedral, Rome, under Donato Bramante. |
| **1508** | Michelangelo started work on the Sistine Chapel fresco in the Vatican. |
| | High Renaissance painter Raphael began decorating the papal apartments. |
| **1509** | Henry VII of England died and was succeeded by son Henry VIII. |
| | Ottoman-held N African port of Oran conquered by Spain. |
| | Dutch humanist Erasmus published *Encomium Moriae/The Praise of Folly*. |
| **1510** | Leonardo da Vinci designed a water turbine. |
| | Netherlandish painter Hieronymous Bosch completed *The Garden of Earthly Delights*. |
| **1511** | Holy League formed against France, including England, Spain, Switzerland, and the Holy Roman Empire. |
| | Portuguese reached Siam. |
| | Portuguese took Malacca. |
| **1512** | War between Russia and Poland (until 1522). |
| | French defeated at Battle of Ravenna and forced to leave Italy. |
| **1513** | Henry VIII defeated French at Battle of Spurs and withdrew from Holy League. |

Battle of Flodden: Scotland defeated and James IV killed.

Florentine political theorist Machiavelli wrote *The Prince*.

---

*One of the most powerful safeguards a prince can have against conspiracies is to avoid being hated by the populace.*
**Niccol Machiavelli**
*The Prince* 1513

---

Spanish conquistador Vasco Balboa saw the Pacific Ocean, having crossed the isthmus of Darien (now Panama).

*1514*          Treaty of Alliance between France and England.

War broke out between Turkey and Persia.

Henry VIII founded Trinity House Corporation of London Pilots.

*1515*          Battle of Chaldiran: Persian armies defeated by Turks.

Hampton Court Palace near London built by Cardinal Wolsey.

Leonardo da Vinci described the *camera obscura*.

---

*They [citizens of Utopia] have but few laws ... but they think it against all right and justice that men should be bound to these laws.*
**Thomas More**
*Utopia* 1516

---

| | |
|---|---|
| **1516** | Syria annexed by Ottoman Empire. |
| | English politician Thomas More wrote *Utopia*. |
| | Michelangelo's *Moses* sculpture completed. |
| **1517** | Cairo conquered by Ottoman Turks. |
| | European traders gained access to China. |
| | Protestant Reformation begun in Germany by Martin Luther when he nailed 95 theses on Wittenberg church door, 31 Oct. |
| **1519** | Charles V elected Holy Roman emperor. |
| | The Reformation began in Switzerland, led by Ulrich Zwingli. |
| **1519–21** | Aztec empire fell to Spanish conquistador Hernán Cortés. |

*I and my companions suffer from a disease of the heart that can be cured only with gold.*
**Hernán Cortés**
Message sent to Montezuma 1519

| | |
|---|---|
| **1519–22** | Portuguese Ferdinand Magellan reached the Philippines by sailing westwards from Spain. |
| | His companions completed the circumnavigation of the Earth. |
| **1520** | Field of the Cloth of Gold: meeting between Henry VIII of England and Francis I of France. |
| | Suleiman the Magnificent became Ottoman sultan of Turkey. |
| | Martin Luther publicly burned at Wittenberg the papal bull that excommunicated him. |
| **1521** | Turks captured Belgrade. |
| | Tatars from Crimea invaded S Russia as far |

as Moscow.

Diet of Worms met to consider Luther's doctrines and condemned him as a heretic. 'My conscience is taken captive by God's word, I cannot and will not recant anything ...'

---

*My conscience is taken captive by God's word, I ccannot and will not recant anything ... Here I stand, I can do no other. God help me. Amen.*
**Martin Luther**
At the Diet of Worms 1521

---

| | |
|---|---|
| *1522* | Turks captured the island of Rhodes. |
| | Martin Luther finished his translation of the New Testament into German. |
| *1522–25* | War between England and France. |
| *1523* | Europeans expelled from China. |
| *1524* | Francisco Pizarro explored coast of South America. |
| | First Lutheran hymn book published. |
| *1526* | Zahir (Babur), great-grandson of Tamerlane, founded Mogul dynasty (to 1858) and conquered most of India. |
| *1527* | Treaty of Amiens between England and France negotiated by Wolsey. |
| | Rome sacked by German and Spanish mercenaries. |
| *1528* | England at war with Holy Roman Empire. |
| | Cocoa beans first brought to Europe. |
| *1529* | Peace of Cambrai concluded on behalf of Francis I of France and Holy Roman emperor |

Charles V.

Henry VIII dismissed Wolsey from chancellorship; Wolsey charged with high treason but died before he could be tried.

Thomas More appointed Lord Chancellor.

Turks unsuccessfully besieged Vienna Sept–Oct.

Treaty of Zaragoza: Spain and Portugal divided up the Far East.

**1530**     Confession of Augsburg, statement of Protestant Faith, presented to Charles V at Diet of Augsburg.

Production of painted enamels on copper began in Limoges, France.

Georgius Agricola began work on his treatise on metallurgy, *De re metallica,* published 1556.

Inquisition established in Portugal.

**1531–33**  Pizarro conquered Peru; Inca king Atahualpa imprisoned and murdered.

**1532**     Henry VIII renounced papal supremacy and declared himself head of the Church of England.

Portuguese began to settle in Brazil.

Turks invaded Hungary but defeated at Göms.

Avoirdupois weight system in use.

**1533**     John Calvin began to establish the Reformation in Paris.

Inca Empire at greatest extent.

Titian, having made his name in Venice, became court painter to Charles V.

Thomas Cranmer made archbishop of Canterbury.

Society of Jesus (Jesuits) founded by Ignatius Loyola.

Martin Luther completed translation of Bible.

Turks captured Baghdad.

French reached Canada.

**1535**	Thomas More executed by Henry VIII for refusing to accept him as head of the church.

Spain annexed Milan.

Pizarro founded the Peruvian city of Lima.

Galápagos Islands reached by Europeans.

**1536**	Union of England and Wales.

Henry VIII executed Anne Boleyn and married Jane Seymour.

French and British began to penetrate Spanish Caribbean.

Hans Holbein's portrait of Henry VIII completed.

**1537**	Jane Seymour died soon after the birth of her son Prince Edward.

Gerardus Mercator produced map of Palestine.

**1538**	Spain conquered Bolivia.

Calvin expelled from Geneva for the severity of his Protestant reforms.

Ottoman Empire annexed North Yemen.

**1539**	Spain annexed Cuba.

**1540**	Spanish explorers reached California.

Henry VIII married Anne of Cleves, then divorced her to marry Catherine Howard.

Thomas Cromwell executed for treason.

Michael Servetus discovered the circulation of

blood through the lungs.

**1541**          Turks conquered Hungary.

John Knox began Reformation in Scotland.

Spanish explorer Pedro de Valdivia conquered Chile and founded Santiago.

**1541–43**      Spanish explorer Francisco Orellana traced the course of the Amazon from Peru to its mouth.

**1542**          England and Scotland at war.

Catherine Howard executed; Henry VIII married Catherine Parr.

Mary Stuart born and acceded to the throne of Scotland at a week old.

**1543**          Copernicus revived the heliocentric ideas of Aristarchus in *De Revolutionibus Orbium Coelestium/About the Revolutions of the Heavenly Spheres*, published the year he died.

---

*Finally we shall place the Sun himself at the centre of the Universe.*
**Nicolaus Copernicus**
*De Revolutionibus Orbium Coelestium* 1543

---

Belgian physician Andreas Vesalius gave the first accurate account of the human body.

Portuguese were the first Europeans to reach Japan.

**1545**          Opening of the Council of Trent: the Counter-Reformation.

**c. 1545**       Silver found in Peru and Mexico.

**1546**          Henry VIII founded the English Navy Board.

Portuguese trade mission sent to Ceylon (Sri Lanka).

Louvre palace rebuilt in Paris.

First accurate map of Britain produced.

**1547**  Henry VIII died; his son Edward VI, a minor, acceded to the throne with Duke of Somerset as Protector.

Ivan IV the Terrible became tsar of Russia.

---

*Did I ascend the throne by robbery or armed bloodshed? I was born to rule by the grace of God ... I grew up upon the throne.*
**Ivan IV the Terrible**
Letter to Prince Kurbsky 1577

---

Venetian Tintoretto painted *The Last Supper.*

**1549**  War broke out between England and France.

Spanish Jesuit missionary Francis Xavier began to preach in Japan.

**1550**  In Germany, Rheticus published trigonometrical tables that simplified calculations involving triangles.

**1551**  Turks took Tripoli in Lebanon.

Nicholas Udall wrote *Ralph Roister Doister,* the first English comedy.

**1552**  Russia conquered Tatar state.

**1553**  Edward VI of England died.

Lady Jane Grey ruled for nine days until accession of Mary Tudor.

**1554**  Lady Jane Grey executed.

| | |
|---|---|
| *1555* | Queen Mary's persecution of Protestants began: bishops Latimer and Ridley burned at the stake in Oxford. |
| *1556* | Accession of Mogul emperor Akbar in India. |
| | Thomas Cranmer, archbishop of Canterbury, burned at the stake. |
| | At least 800,000 people killed in earthquake in China. |
| *1558* | Mary I of England died; Elizabeth Tudor succeeded as Elizabeth I. |
| | French entered Senegal. |
| *1559* | Acts of Supremacy and Uniformity restored Protestant Church in England. |
| *1562* | French Wars of Religion (until 1598). |
| *1563* | Sweden and Denmark at war. |
| *1564* | War between England and Spain broke out. |
| | Period of Terror introduced by Tsar Ivan IV. |
| | The violin was designed and manufactured by Andrea Amati in Cremona. |
| | William Shakespeare was born. |
| *1565* | Spanish settled Florida. |
| | Spain conquered the Philippines. |
| | Turkish attack on Malta failed. |
| *1566* | Suleiman the Magnificent died. |
| | Exchanges established in London, Cologne, and Rouen. |
| *1567* | Portuguese founded Rio de Janeiro. |
| | Mary Queen of Scots forced to abdicate. |
| *1568* | Dutch revolt against Spanish rule began; Spanish Inquisition condemned to death as |

heretics all inhabitants of the Netherlands.

Kyoto taken by Oda Nobunaga, the first of three great warlords who unified Japan.

El Greco in Spain painted *Coronation of a Saint or a King*.

Mercator navigational chart invented.

**1570**      Elizabeth I excommunicated.

War broke out between Sweden and Denmark.

**1571**      Ottoman Turks captured Cyprus and Tunis.

Battle of Lepanto: defeat of Ottoman Empire by fleets of Venice, Genoa, Spain, and Papal States, led by Don John of Austria.

Moscow burned by khan of Crimea.

**1572**      French invasion of Netherlands; William of Orange became stadholder.

Massacre of St Bartholomew: some 25,000 French Huguenots (Protestants) killed at instigation of Catherine de' Medici.

**1573**      Last Ashikaga shogun deposed by Nobunaga in Japan.

**1574**      Portuguese began colonizing Angola.

**1575**      Akbar conquered Bengal.

English composers Thomas Tallis and William Byrd jointly published their *Cantiones sacrae*, a collection of 34 motets.

**c. 1576**   The first English playhouse, the Theatre, was built by James Burbage in London.

**1576**      English navigator Martin Frobisher explored N Canada looking for the Northwest Passage.

Hans Sachs, foremost of the Meistersinger

('master singer') poets and composers, died in Nuremberg.

Danish astronomer Tycho Brahe established observatory on an island in the Sound.

**1577–81**    Francis Drake in the *Pelican* (later *Golden Hind*) made the first journey of an English subject around the world.

**1579**    United Provinces (Dutch) proclaimed independence from Spain in Union of Utrecht.

**1580**    Spain conquered Portugal.

Death of Wu Ch'eng-en, author of classic Chinese picaresque novel *Monkey*.

**1581**    Russians began conquest of Siberia.

Akbar conquered Afghanistan.

The first dramatic ballet was staged in Paris.

**1582**    Poland waged a successful campaign against Russia.

**1583**    Galileo Galilei in Pisa discovered that each oscillation of a pendulum takes the same time despite the difference in amplitude.

**1584**    Tsar Ivan IV died; succeeded by son Fyodor.

William I of Orange assassinated.

English adventurer Walter Raleigh annexed Virginia.

**1585**    Elizabeth I began war with Spain.

Toyotomi Hideyoshi, the second great Japanese warlord, appointed regent.

**1587**    Mary Queen of Scots executed.

Akbar captured Kashmir.

Christopher Marlowe's play *Tamburlaine the*

|  |  |
|---|---|
|  | *Great* marked the beginning of the great age of Elizabethan and Jacobean drama in England. |
| *1588* | English defeated Spanish Armada. |
| *1589* | Bourbon dynasty began in France. |
|  | Thomas Kyd's play *Spanish Tragedy* was the first of the revenge tragedies. |
| *c. 1590* | Akbar conquered Orissa. |
| *c. 1590–1612* | Shakespeare wrote his greatest plays, including *Hamlet* and *King Lear.* |
| *1591* | Morocco conquered Songhai Empire. |
| *1592* | Hideyoshi's invasion of Korea repelled. |
|  | Akbar conquered Sind. |
|  | Presbyterian system of church government founded in Scotland. |
|  | English explorer John Davis was the first European to visit the Falkland Islands. |
|  | Christopher Marlowe's *The Tragicall History of Dr Faustus* produced. |
| *1593* | Playwright Christopher Marlowe murdered in a tavern. |
| *1595* | Franco-Spanish War began. |
| *1596* | Francis Drake died at sea in the West Indies. |
|  | Tomatoes introduced into England. |
| *1597* | Second Spanish Armada sent to England destroyed by storms. |
|  | The first opera, *La Dafne* by Jacopo Peri, was staged privately at the Corsi Palazzo in Florence. |
| *1598* | *The Edict of Nantes* issued by Henry IV of France allowed Protestants to worship according to their faith. |

We *permit those of the so-called Reformed Religion to live and abide in all the towns and districts of this our realm ... free from inquisition, molestation or compulsion to do anything ... against their Conscience.*
**Henry IV of France**
*The Edict of Nantes* 1598

Tsar Fyodor died; Boris Godunov elected tsar; time of civil disturbances began in Russia.

Hideyoshi died.

Thomas Bodley began to rebuild the library at Oxford.

**1599**    Akbar began conquest of the Deccan plateau of India.

Globe Theatre built at Southwark, London.

**1600**    English East India Company formed.

Victory in the Battle of Sekigahara gave warlord Tokugawa Ieyasu virtual control of Japan.

Magnetism was described by English scientist William Gilbert.

Giordano Bruno, Italian philosopher, burned at the stake for heresy by the Inquisition.

**1601**    Poor Relief Act passed in England.

**1602**    Dutch East India Company formed.

**1602–18**  Turkey and Persia at war.

**1603**    Elizabeth I died; James IV of Scotland acceded to throne of England as James I.

Tokugawa shogunate established in Edo (Tokyo).

|       |                                                                                          |
|-------|------------------------------------------------------------------------------------------|
|       | Kabuki theatre began in Kyoto.                                                            |
| *1604* | French East India Company founded.                                                      |
|       | Inigo Jones designed *The Masque of Blackness*, written by Ben Jonson, for James I.       |
| *1605* | French settled in Nova Scotia.                                                           |
|       | England claimed Barbados.                                                                 |
|       | Gunpowder Plot to blow up Houses of Parliament uncovered; Guy Fawkes executed.            |
|       | Akbar died; succeeded by his son Salim.                                                   |
|       | Miguel Cervantes' novel *Don Quixote* was published in Spain.                             |

---

*There are only two families in the world, as an old grandmother of mine used to say: the Haves and the Have-nots.*
**Miguel de Cervantes Saavedra**
*Don Quixote*

---

|       |                                                                                          |
|-------|------------------------------------------------------------------------------------------|
| *1606* | First European sighting of Australia, from a Dutch ship.                                 |
|       | Luis Vaez Torres navigated through the strait between New Guinea and Australia.            |
|       | Flemish painter Peter Paul Rubens created *The Circumcision* altarpiece in Genoa.         |
| *1607* | English founded Jamestown, Virginia, their first permanent settlement in North America.  |
|       | War broke out between Sweden and Poland.                                                  |
| *1608* | Québec founded by French explorer Samuel de Champlain.                                   |
|       | Dutch lensmaker Hans Lippershey invented the                                              |

refracting telescope.

**1609**          Portugal took Ceylon (Sri Lanka) from Dutch.

Spanish defeated Turkish fleet at Tunis.

English explorer Henry Hudson reached New York Bay and sailed up the river now named after him.

Galileo developed an astronomical telescope and observed craters on the Moon.

Johann Kepler's first two laws of planetary motion were published (the third appeared 1619).

**1610**          Henry Hudson entered what is now the Hudson Strait and was set adrift in the following year in what is now Hudson Bay.

The principle of falling bodies descending to earth at the same speed was established by Galileo.

---

*In questions of science the authority of a thousand is not worth the humble reasoning of a single individual.*
**Galileo**

---

Composer Monteverdi's *Vespers* was published in Venice.

Ben Jonson's play *The Alchemist* was first performed.

**1611**          First Parliament of James I dissolved.

James I's Authorized Version of the Bible published.

**1613**          Beginning of Romanov dynasty in Russia.

Manhattan settled by Dutch.

**1614** James I's Addled Parliament met.

Walter Raleigh's *History of the World*, written while he was imprisoned in the Tower of London, published.

Scottish mathematician John Napier invented logarithms.

Lope de Vega's *Fuenteovejuna* marked the Spanish renaissance in drama; other writers include Calderón de la Barca.

**1615** Champlain reached the Canadian Great Lakes.

Tribes in N China started forming military groupings, later called Manchus.

English architect Inigo Jones appointed surveyor-general of the royal buildings.

**1616** With Robert Bylot, William Baffin explored Baffin Bay, Canada.

Cape Horn rounded by Dutch explorer Willem Schouten; cape named after his birthplace Hoorn.

Christianity proscribed in Japan.

**1618** Outbreak of Thirty Years' War in Germany, which spread throughout central Europe.

Walter Raleigh executed for treason.

**1619** First American legislature in Virginia.

First black slaves landed in an English colony (Virginia).

Dutch empire founded in East Indies.

Inigo Jones began work on New Palace in Whitehall.

**1620**          *Mayflower* arrived in New England; Pilgrims settled in Massachusetts.

Dutch engineer Cornelius Drebbel invented the submarine.

Scientific method of reasoning expounded by English philosopher Francis Bacon in his *Novum Organum*.

---

*There is nothing makes a man suspect much, more than to know little.*
**Francis Bacon**
*Of Suspicion*

---

**1621**          Third Parliament of James I.

Iraq re-occupied by Persia.

Dutch West India Company founded.

Dutch took over Guyana.

Sweden conquered N Latvia; remainder already divided between Poland and Lithuania.

Willebrord Snell devised Snell's law, the basic law of refraction of light.

**1622**          Third Parliament of James I dissolved.

English mathematician William Oughtred invented the slide rule.

The process for making coke from coal patented in England.

**1623**          Colonies of Maine and New Hampshire first settled.

Wilhelm Schickard invented the mechanical calculating machine.

Blaise Pascal, French philosopher and mathematician, born.

*1624*    Fourth Parliament of James I.

Dutch-Portuguese wars over Brazil (until 1654).

Virginia became a crown colony.

Surveyor's chain invented by Edmund Gunter.

Henry Briggs introduced base-ten logarithms.

Flemish Frans Hals painted *The Laughing Cavalier.*

*1625*    James I died; succeeded by Charles I.

Protestant Denmark entered Thirty Years' War.

Dutch founded New Amsterdam (New York).

French founded Cayenne in Guiana.

Sweden annexed Estonia.

Dutch lawyer Hugo Grotius wrote *De Jure Belli et Pacis/On the Law of War and Peace*, the foundation of international law.

*1626*    Swedish forces under Gustavus Adolphus defeated Poles in Battle of Wallhof.

*1627*    England at war with France.

England secured Barbados.

Korea became a tributary state of China.

Johannes Kepler published his astronomical *Rudolphine Tables.*

*1628*    English physician William Harvey described the circulation of the blood and the function of the heart as a pump in *De Motu Cordis/On the Motion of the Heart and the Blood in Animals.*

*1629*    English army took Québec from French.

*1630*    Great migration to the New World began.

English and French made claims on West Indies possessions.

Protestant Sweden entered Thirty Years' War.

Construction of the Taj Mahal near Agra, India, began.

**1631**     Naples struck by earthquake.

French mathematician Pierre Vernier published *La construction, l'usage, et les propitez du quadrant nouveau mathematique/The construction/uses, and properties of a new mathematical quadrant*, in which he explained a method of making very precise measurements.

The square of Covent Garden laid out by Inigo Jones.

**1632**     Portuguese withdrew from Bengal.

The world's first official observatory was established in Leiden in the Netherlands.

**1633**     Portuguese expelled from Abyssinian territory.

Galileo's heliocentric theories were condemned by the Inquisition.

**1634**     English Catholics founded Maryland.

Charles I attempted to levy ship money, a tax to support the navy, on whole country (to 1636).

**1635**     French entered Thirty Years' War against Spain.

Colony of Connecticut founded by Puritans from Massachusetts.

**1636**     Japan isolated itself from the rest of the world (until 1853).

Colony of Rhode Island founded by Roger Williams.

Harvard University founded at New Towne

(later Cambridge), Massachusetts.

**1637**   French invaded Netherlands.

Russian explorers reached Pacific coast.

French settlements set up in Senegal.

Pierre Corneille's *Le Cid* established classical tragedy in France.

---

*When there is no peril in the fight, there is no glory in the triumph.*
**Pierre Corneille**
*Le Cid*

---

The world's first opera house opened in Venice.

French mathematician and philosopher René Descartes introduced co-ordinate geometry.

**1637–38**   Shimabara rebellion of Christian converts ended in mass slaughter; last time guns used in battle in Japan for more than two centuries.

**1638**   Dutch took Mauritius.

**1639**   Dutch took Trincomalee in Ceylon (Sri Lanka) from Portuguese.

**1640**   Anglo-Scottish war renewed.

Portugal and Catalonia rebelled against Spain.

**1641**   Revolt began in Ireland against English rule.
Dutch ousted Portuguese from Malacca.

English Star Chamber court abolished.

French settled in Michigan.

**1642**   Start of English Civil War between Parliamentarians (under Oliver Cromwell) and Royalists (under Charles I).

Battle of Edgehill indecisive.

Dutch navigator Abel Tasman landed at Van Diemen's Land (Tasmania).

The principles of hydraulics were put forward by French mathematician Blaise Pascal.

---

*The heart has its reasons which reason knows nothing of.*
**Blaise Pascal**
*Pensées*

---

Montréal founded in Canada.

Dutch artist Rembrandt painted group portrait *The Night Watch.*

An act of Parliament closed all English theatres.

English scientist Isaac Newton was born.

**1643** End of Ming dynasty in China.

Tasman visited Friendly Islands (Tonga).

The mercury barometer was invented in Italy by Evangelista Torricelli.

**1644** Battle of Marston Moor: Cromwell's army defeated Prince Rupert's Royalists.

Qing (Manchu) dynasty established in China.

Antonio Stradivarius was born. More than 600 of his violins, made in Cremona, survived into the 20th century.

**1645** Battle of Naseby: Cromwell and his commander in chief, Thomas Fairfax, defeated Charles I's army.

Turkey at war with Venice over Crete.

Blaise Pascal produced a calculator.

*1646* Charles I surrendered to Scottish army at Newark.

*1647* Scots gave up Charles I to English Parliament.

*1648* Royalist and Presbyterian uprising defeated by Cromwell's New Model Army.

Treaty of Westphalia ended Thirty Years' War, which left Germany devastated.

*1649* Charles I executed: Britain a republic (to 1660).

Cromwell invaded Ireland and crushed revolt.

First frigate, *Constant Warwick*, built for English navy.

*1650* Cromwell defeated Royalists under future Charles II at Dunbar, Scotland.

French began colonizing Canada.

Rise of Ashanti people in W Africa.

Commonwealth Ordinance forbade foreign ships to trade in English colonies.

Death of French philosopher and mathematician Réné Descartes.

Leiden University in the Netherlands set up the first chemistry laboratory.

*1651* Cromwell defeated Royalists at Battle of Worcester; future Charles II fled to France.

English political philosopher Thomas Hobbes published *The Leviathan*, in which he advocated absolute goverment to ensure order.

Navigation Act in England prohibited any goods to be imported in vessels not either English or from country of origin of goods.

| | |
|---|---|
| **1652** | Dutch founded Cape Colony in southern Africa. |
| | First Anglo-Dutch war resulted from Navigation Act. |
| **1653** | Cromwell expelled Parliament and was appointed Lord Protector. |

---

*A few honest men are better than numbers.*
**Oliver Cromwell**
Letter 1643

---

| | |
|---|---|
| | Izaak Walton's classic fishing textbook *Compleat Angler* published in England. |
| **1654** | First Anglo-Dutch war ended. |
| | Portuguese drove Dutch from Brazil. |
| | Poland at war with Russia and Sweden. |
| | In France, Blaise Pascal and Pierre de Fermat developed probability theory. |
| **1655** | English took Jamaica from Spanish. |
| | Diego Velázquez painted *Las Meninas/The Ladies-in- Waiting* at the Spanish court. |
| **1656** | Anglo-Spanish war. |
| | The pendulum clock was invented by Dutch physicist Christiaan Huygens. |
| **1657** | Dutch Republic and Portuguese at war. |
| | Charles X of Sweden led army across frozen sea to Denmark. |
| **1658** | Dutch took over rule of Ceylon (Sri Lanka) from Portuguese. |
| | Aurangzeb became Mogul emperor in India. |
| | Oliver Cromwell died; succeeded by his son |

Richard as Lord Protector.

**1659** Treaty of Pyrenees ended Franco-Spanish war.

English bureaucrat Samuel Pepys began his diary.

**1660** Charles II restored in England.

---

*This is very true: for my words are my own, and my actions are my ministers'.*
**Charles II**
In reply to Lord Rochester's observation that the king 'never said a foolish thing nor ever did a wise one'

---

Dramatic performances recommenced in England; the first professional actress appeared as Desdemona in Shakespeare's *Othello*.

English Royal Society granted its charter.

**1661** Turkey and Holy Roman Empire at war.

Irish chemist Robert Boyle gave scientific definition of an element, postulating the existence of atoms.

Bank of Sweden issued banknotes, the first in the world.

**1662** Boyle formulated his law concerning the behaviour of gases.

Bombay came under administration of English East India Company.

**1663** Colony of North Carolina established.

**1664** Second Anglo-Dutch war broke out: English seized New Amsterdam from Dutch; New Jersey ceded to England by Dutch.

French East India Company formed.

French landscape artist Claude Lorrain painted *The Enchanted Castle* in Rome.

French playwright Molière's *Tartuffe* was banned for three years by religious factions.

---

*It is a public scandal that gives offence, and it is no sin to sin in secret.*
**Molière**
*Tartuffe*

---

**1665**

Battle of Ambuila: Portuguese killed king of the Congo kingdom.

English defeated Dutch fleet at Lowestoft.

Isaac Newton put forward the law of gravity, stating that the Earth exerts a constant force on falling bodies.

English scientist Robert Hooke used a microscope to describe the cellular structure of plants.

Great Plague of London killed quarter of population.

**1666**

France declared war on England.

Isaac Newton developed differential calculus, a method of calculating rates of change.

Great Fire of London began in Pudding Lane; the Gothic St Paul's Cathedral destroyed.

**1667**

Treaty of Breda: Anglo-Dutch war ended.

New Amsterdam renamed New York.

Jean Racine's first success, *Andromaque*, was staged.

John Milton's epic poem *Paradise Lost* published.

---

*The mind has its own place and in itself / Can make a heaven of hell, a hell of heaven.*
**John Milton**
*Paradise Lost* 1667

---

| | |
|---|---|
| *1667–68* | War of Devolution: unsuccessful attempt by France to gain Spanish territory in the Netherlands. |
| *1668* | Triple Alliance of England, Netherlands, and Sweden against France. |
| | Treaty of Lisbon: Spain recognized Portugal's independence. |
| | England acquired Bombay. |
| *1669* | Hindus persecuted in India by Aurangzeb. |
| | Pepys' diary ended. |
| *1670* | Secret Treaty of Dover between England and France. |
| | Hudson's Bay Company founded. |
| | Pascal wrote his *Pensées*. |
| | Newton built first reflecting telescope. |
| | Probable extinction of the dodo on Mauritius. |
| *1671* | Work began on Hôtel des Invalides, a hospital for the care of old soldiers in Paris. |
| *1672* | Third Anglo-Dutch war broke out. |
| | German mathematician Gottfried Wilhelm Leibniz built his first calculator, the stepped reckoner. |

Marcello Malpighi undertook the first studies in embryology by describing the development of a chicken egg.

Violinist John Banister pioneered public concerts in London.

**1674** Treaty of Westminster: third Anglo-Dutch war ended.

Maratha kingdom in India invaded.

**1675** Royal Greenwich Observatory founded in England.

Leibniz introduced the modern notation for integral calculus, a method of calculating volumes.

John Bunyan began writing *Pilgrim's Progress* while in prison.

Work began on the building of London's new St Paul's Cathedral, designed by Christopher Wren.

The Baroque style had spread from Rome throughout Europe.

Royal Greenwich Observatory founded to provide navigational information for sailors.

Death of Dutch painter Jan Vermeer in Delft.

**1676** Sikh uprisings in India.

**1677** The simple microscope was invented in Delft by Anton van Leeuwenhoek.

**1678–79** Treaties of Nijmegen ended the Third Dutch War (France against the Netherlands, Spain, and the Holy Roman Empire).

**1679** Leibniz introduced binary arithmetic, in which only two symbols are used to represent all numbers.

*1680*    The Comédie Franaise was formed by Louis XIV.

*1681*    Pennsylvania colony founded by Quakers.

Louis XIV of France seized Strasbourg in Alsace. First streetlamps in London.

*1682*    Peter I the Great became tsar of Russia.

Louisiana explored by La Salle and claimed for France.

Spanish settled in Texas.

English astronomer Edmond Halley observed the comet later to be named after him.

Nehemiah Grew published the first textbook in botany.

Chelsea Royal Hospital for old and disabled soldiers founded.

*1683*    Peace treaty between William Penn and North American Indians.

Turkey's defeat at Vienna ended advance of Islam into Europe.

Taiwan (Formosa) incorporated into China.

*1684*    Leibniz published the first account of differential calculus.

*De Motu corporum in gyrum/On the motion of bodies in orbit* written by Isaac Newton.

*1685*    Charles II of England died; succeeded by James II.

Edict of Nantes revoked; Huguenot exodus from France.

All Chinese ports opened to foreign trade.

| | |
|---|---|
| *1686* | Mogul emperor Aurangzeb annexed Indian kingdom of Biafra. |
| *1687* | Isaac Newton's *Principia,* was published, including his law of universal gravitation'. |
| *1688* | Glorious Revolution in England: William of Orange offered English crown by opponents of James II. |
| | War of the League of Augsburg (France against Grand Alliance). |
| | Marine insurance headquarters established in Edward Lloyd's coffee house in Tower Street, London. |
| *1689* | William III of Orange and Mary II crowned King and Queen of England. |
| | Declaration of Rights ensured British monarchs ruled with the consent of Parliament. |
| | Treaty of Nerchinsk between China and Russia over boundaries. |
| *1690* | Battle of the Boyne in Ireland: James II defeated by William III. |
| | Mogul conquests of S India almost complete. |
| | The wave theory of light was propounded by Christiaan Huygens. |
| *1692* | Glencoe Massacre of clan Macdonald by John Campbell in Scotland. |
| | Edict of Toleration for Roman Catholics in China. |
| *1693* | China invaded Mongolia. |
| *1694* | Bank of England founded by act of Parliament. |
| *1695* | Russo-Turkish war began. |
| *1696* | British engineer Thomas Savery invented steam- |

driven water pump.

*1697*           French gained Haiti.

Peace of Ryswick marked defeat of France by Grand Alliance.

German chemist Georg Stahl proposed the erroneous theory that substances ·burn because they are rich in a certain substance, called phlogiston.

*1699*           Turks lost Hungary to Austria.

Sultanate of Oman established on east coast of Africa.

French began to colonize Louisiana.

*1700*           Great Northern War (until 1721) between Russia and Sweden began.

British East India Company took control of key Indian ports.

William Congreve, the greatest exponent of English Restoration comedy, wrote *The Way of the World*.

*1701*           Act of Settlement in England established Protestant Hanoverian succession.

James II of England died.

War of the Spanish Succession broke out.

Jethro Tull in England developed a mechanical seed drill.

*Irises* painted on pair of screens by Ogata Kōrin in Japan.

*1702*           French settled in Alabama.

*1703*           Work began on the building of Buckingham Palace for the Duke of Buckingham.

Japan's greatest playwright, Chikamatsu Monzaemon, wrote *Sonezaki shinju/The Love Suicides of Sonezaki* for the bunraku puppet theatre in Osaka.

**1704**      Britain captured Gibraltar.

The corpuscular theory of light was put forward by Isaac Newton.

**1705**      Thomas Newcomen in England patented the first steam engine.

**1707**      Act of Union of England and Scotland.

Death of Mogul emperor Aurangzeb: power struggle in India to 1761.

**1709**      Battle of Poltava: Peter the Great defeated Charles XII of Sweden.

Bartolommeo Cristofori built the first piano in Florence.

**1710**      British captured Nova Scotia from French.

Estonia and N Latvia came under Russian control.

**1711**      Russo-Turkish war broke out.

French captured Rio de Janeiro.

English poet and satirist Alexander Pope published *Essay on Criticism*.

**1713**      British gained Newfoundland and Hudson Bay.

Treaty of Utrecht ended Louis XIV's expansionism; Britain gained Gibraltar; the Bourbon dynasty came to the throne of Spain; Spain lost its possessions in Italy and the Netherlands.

Russo-Turkish war renewed.

**1714**      Tripoli gained independence from Turkey.

Treaty of Rastatt between Austria and France ended War of Spanish Succession.

The mercury thermometer was invented by Gabriel Fahrenheit.

*1715*    Jacobite rising in Scotland.

*1716*    The first known American theatre was built in Williamsburg, Virginia.

*1717*    Lady Mary Wortley Montagu, society hostess, introduced inoculation against smallpox into Britain.

Rococo painter Jean-Antoine Watteau won membership of the French Academy with *The Embarkation of Cythera*.

*1718*    England declared war on Spain.

Jakob Bernoulli in Switzerland published his work on the calculus of variations (the study of functions that are close to their minimum or maximum values).

*1719*    Spain invaded Scotland to support Jacobites.

France declared war on Spain.

Austrian composer Wolfgang Amadeus Mozart born.

Daniel Defoe's *Robinson Crusoe* published.

---

*Necessity makes an honest man a knave.*
**Daniel Defoe**
*Serious Reflections of Robinson Crusoe*

---

*1720*    South Sea Bubble financial crisis in Britain.
Chinese invaded Tibet.

| | |
|---|---|
| *1721* | Proclamation of the Russian Empire. |
| | German composer J S Bach completed his six Brandenburg Concertos. |
| *1722* | Jean-Philippe Rameau's book *Traité de l'harmonie* founded modern harmonic theory. |
| *1725* | Treaty of Vienna (Pragmatic Sanction) united Austrian Habsburgs and Spanish Bourbons. |
| | Peter the Great of Russia died; succeeded by Catherine I. |
| | Italian composer Antonio Vivaldi's *The Four Seasons* was published in Amsterdam. |
| *1726* | Irish satirist Jonathan Swift's novel *Gulliver's Travels* published. |
| *1727* | Spanish siege of Gibraltar; war between Britain and Spain. |
| *1728* | John Gay's *The Beggar's Opera* was first performed in England. |
| *1729* | Arabs took Mombasa on the east coast of Africa from Portugal. |
| *1730* | John and Charles Wesley founded Methodist Society at Oxford. |
| | Réné Réaumur developed the alcohol thermometer. |
| | John Hadley invented a navigational instrument, the sextant. |
| *1731* | Treaty of Vienna (England, Holland, Spain, and Holy Roman Emperor). |
| *1732* | Covent Garden Theatre opened in London. |
| | (It was later destroyed twice by fire, 1808 and 1856, but rebuilt.) |
| *1733* | Georgia became the 13th British crown colony |

in the New World.

*1734* Turko-Persian war broke out.

*1735* Chinese expanded into Turkistan, Annam (Vietnam), Burma, and Nepal.

English lawyer George Hadley described the circulation of the atmosphere as large-scale convection currents centred on the equator.

William Hogarth completed *A Rake's Progress*, a series of engravings.

*1736* Russo-Turkish war.

Swede Carolus Linnaeus (Carl von Linné) published his systematic classification of plants, so establishing taxonomy.

---

*Nature does not make jumps.*
**Carolus Linnaeus**
*Philosophia Botanica* 1751

---

*1737* The Stage Licensing Act in England required all plays to be approved by the Lord Chamberlain before performance.

*1739* War of Jenkins's Ear between Britain and Spain arose from Britain's illicit trade in South America.

Persians pillaged Delhi.

New Granada parted from Peru.

*1739–40* Scottish philosopher David Hume published *A Treatise on Human Nature*, a central text of British empiricism.

*1739–41* Famine in Ireland killed one-third of population.

*1740* Accessions of Frederick II the Great of Prussia

and Maria Theresa of Austria.

War of the Austrian Succession began.

Canaletto painted *The Square of St Mark's in Venice.*

---

*My people and I have come to an agreement which satisfies us both.They are to say what they please and I am to do what I please.*
**Frederick II the Great**
(attributed)

---

| | |
|---|---|
| **1742** | Georg Friedrich Handel's *Messiah* received its world premiere in Dublin. |
| **1743** | Christopher Packe produced the first geological map, of S England. |
| **1744** | France declared war on Britain and Austria. |
| | The first map produced on modern surveying principles was produced by César-François Cassini in France. |
| **1745** | Peace of Dresden: Prussia recognized Pragmatic Sanction of 1725. |
| | Last Jacobite uprising in Britain. |
| | In Russia, Mikhail Vasilievich Lomonosov published a catalogue of over 3,000 minerals. |
| **1746** | Battle of Culloden: Jacobite rebellion defeated in Scotland. |
| | In France, Jean le Rond d'Alembert developed the theory of complex numbers. |
| | A French expedition to Lapland proved the Earth to be flattened at the poles. |
| **1747** | Afghanistan united. |

D'Alembert used partial differential equations in mathematical physics.

**1748** War of the Austrian Succession concluded.

The buried Roman city of Pompeii was discovered under lava from Vesuvius.

**1749** English writer Henry Fielding's novel *Tom Jones* published.

---

*His designs were strictly honourable, as the phrase is; that is, to rob a lady of her fortune by marrying her.*
**Henry Fielding**
*Tom Jones*

---

**1750** Spanish-Portuguese treaty over South America.

Ngwane III conquered Swaziland.

Fall of Toungoo dynasty in Burma (Myanmar).

**1751** Britain captured Arcot, India, from French.

China invaded Tibet.

Publication in France of first volume of the *Encyclopédie*, a 28-volume encyclopedia that spread the views of the Enlightenment.

**1752** Burma reunited under Alaungpaya, who founded Rangoon (Yangon).

**1754** Scottish chemist Joseph Black discovered carbon dioxide.

Royal and Ancient Golf Club founded in St Andrews, Scotland; it is the ruling body of the sport.

**1755** Lisbon devastated by earthquake.

Samuel Johnson's *Dictionary of the English Language* published.

**1756**    Seven Years' War (French and Indian War) began: Britain declared war on France over colonial supremacy; other European powers also in conflict.

British soldiers died in Black Hole of Calcutta.

**1757**    Battle of Plassey: Britain defeated nawab of Bengal.

---

*With the loss of twenty-two soldiers killed and fifty wounded, Clive had scattered an enemy of nearly sixty thousand men, and subdued an empire larger and more populous than Great Britain.*
**Lord Macauley**
On the Battle of Plassey

---

Johann Stamitz died in Mannheim, where he had founded the world's first virtuoso orchestra.

**1758**    British conquered French Canada.

**1759**    General James Wolfe commanded British forces that captured Québec. China occupied E Turkestan.

Royal Botanic Gardens, Kew, founded.

**1760**    French defeated in India, leaving British supreme.

John Mitchell proposed that earthquakes are produced when one layer of rock rubs against another.

Lloyd's Register of Shipping founded.

Irish experimental novelist Laurence Sterne began writing *The Life and Opinions of Tristram Shandy, Gent.*

*1761*   Britain gained control of West Indies.

Battle of Panipat ended Maratha attempt to dominate India.

Austrian composer Franz Joseph Haydn took up liveried service as vice kapellmeister with the aristocratic Esterházy family, with whom he was connected until his death in 1809.

*1762*   Accession of Catherine II (the Great) as empress of Russia.

---

*I shall be an autocrat: that's my trade. And the good Lord will forgive me: that's his.*
**Catherine II**
(attributed)

---

Britain declared war on Spain.

Publication of *Social Contract* by French philosopher Jean-Jacques Rousseau; its emphasis on the rights of the people was to influence the French Revolution.

*1763*   Peace of Paris ended Seven Years' War: France lost American possessions to Britain.

Ottawa Indians fought British.

Rio de Janeiro became capital of Brazil. Death of Cao Chan, author of *Hung Lou Meng/The Dream of the Red Chamber,* a classic Chinese novel of manners.

*1764*   James Hargreaves invented his spinning jenny.

Specific and latent heats were described by Joseph Black.

1765    Britain imposed Stamp Act on American colonies.

British battleship *HMS Victory* launched; later Nelson's flagship.

1766    The fossilized bones of a huge animal (later called Mosasaurus) were found in a quarry near the river Meuse, the Netherlands.

English physicist Henry Cavendish discovered hydrogen: 'inflammable air'.

Mason-Dixon line established as boundary between Maryland and Pennsylvania.

1767    First Mysore War fought against East India Company forces.

1768    Turkey declared war on Russia.

Scottish anatomist John Hunter began the foundation of experimental and surgical pathology.

English explorer James Cook landed in New Zealand and on east coast of Australia.

English manufacturer Richard Arkwright invented a spinning frame for spinning cotton.

*Encyclopaedia Britannica* first appeared.

English portrait painter Joshua Reynolds became the first president of the Royal Academy.

1769    Burmese recognized Chinese sovereignty.

Napoleon Bonaparte born in Corsica.

Scottish engineer James Watt made significant improvements to the steam engine.

Nicholas-Joseph Cugnot in France built a

steam tractor.

**1770**  Cook claimed New South Wales as a British colony.

Scottish explorer James Bruce discovered source of the Blue Nile.

The link between nerve action and electricity was discovered by Italian Luigi Galvani.

Swedish chemist Karl Wilhelm Scheele discovered oxygen.

The first cotton-spinning factory set up in England.

**1772**  First partition of Poland by Russia and Prussia.

Daniel Rutherford isolated nitrogen.

**1773**  Boston Tea Party: in protest against tea tax imposed by Britain, a valuable consignment of tea was thrown overboard in Boston harbour.

In England, Oliver Goldsmith's *She Stoops to Conquer* and Richard Sheridan's *The Rivals* (1775) established the 'comedy of manners'.

Goethe's *Götz von Berlichingen* was the first *Sturm und Drang* play (an early Romantic movement in literature).

Bode's law gave approximate distances of planets from the Sun.

**1774**  Turkey left Crimea.

English chemist Joseph Priestley discovered oxygen, which he called 'dephlogisticated air'.

French chemist Antoine Lavoisier demonstrated his law of conservation of mass.

Portrait painter Thomas Gainsborough arrived in London from Bath.

The rules of cricket were first drawn up.

**1775-83**   First Maratha War in India.

American Revolution began with fighting at Lexington and Concord, Massachusetts.

**1776**   American Declaration of Independence issued on 4 July.

Viceroyalty of River Plate founded in South America.

Dutch Afrikaners met Bantu.

US engineer David Bushnell built a hand-powered submarine, Turtle, with buoyancy tanks.

The Bolshoi Ballet was established in Moscow.

Edward Gibbon began *The History of the Decline and Fall of the Roman Empire*.

**1777**   The first boat with an iron hull was built in Yorkshire, England.

Lavoisier showed air to be made up of a mixture of gases, and showed that one of these – oxygen – is the substance necessary for combustion (burning) and rusting to take place.

**1778**   France and Spain supported America in the War of Independence.

**1779**   French naturalist Comte George de Buffon speculated that the Earth may be much older than the 6,000 years suggested by the Bible.

Samuel Crompton built spinning mule, another step in the Industrial Revolution in Britain.

**1780**   Peruvian Indians revolted against Spanish.

Second Mysore War.

**1781**   Battle of Yorktown in American Revolution.

Henry Cavendish showed water to be a compound.

Friedrich von Schiller's play *Die Räuber/The Robbers* successful in Germany.

German-born astronomer William Herschel in England discovered Uranus and recognized stellar systems beyond our galaxy.

German philosopher Immanuel Kant published *Kritik der reinen Vernunft/Critique of Pure Reason.*

*1782* Anna Godi became the last woman officially to be executed as a witch in Europe.

*1783* American Revolution ended by Treaty of Paris.

Russia annexed Crimea.

First human flight, by Jean F Pilâtre de Rozier and the Marquis d'Arlandes, in Paris, using a hot-air balloon made by Joseph and Etienne Montgolfier; first ascent in a hydrogen-filled balloon by Jacques Charles and M N Robert in Paris.

Frenchman Jouffroy d'Abbans built the first paddle-driven steamboat.

*1784* USA began trade with China.

Thomas Jefferson excavated an Indian burial mound on the Rivanna River in Virginia and wrote a report on his finds.

India Act.

French dramatist Beaumarchais' comedy *Le Mariage de Figaro/The Marriage of Figaro* (written 1778) was first performed.

French painter Jacques Louis David produced

*The Oath of the Horatii.*

**1785**      Burma conquered kingdom of Arakan.

Jean-Pierre Blanchard and John J Jeffries made the first balloon crossing of the English Channel.

Scottish geologist James Hutton proposed the theory of uniformitarianism: all geological features are the result of processes that are at work today, acting over long periods of time.

Dollar adopted as standard monetary unit in USA.

Charles Coulomb devised inverse square law.

**1786**      British took Malacca in what is now peninsular Malaysia.

German-Swiss Johann von Carpentier described the European ice age.

**1787**      US constitution adopted.

Turkey declared war on Russia.

French physicist Jacques Charles formulated law relating the pressure, volume, and temperature of a gas.

Marylebone Cricket Club formed in London; established current rules for cricket.

**1788**      Colonization of Australia began at Botany Bay.

Mozart completed his last three symphonies, numbers 39–41, in six weeks.

**1789**      States General (French parliament) summoned for the first time since 1614. Commons (third estate) then formed national assembly.

French Revolution began; Bastille prison stormed by demonstrators on 14 July.

George Washington elected first US president.

*There is nothing so likely to produce peace as to be well prepared to meet an enemy.*
**George Washington**
Letter 1780

English poet William Blake's *Songs of Innocence* published.

English naturalist Gilbert White's *Natural History and Antiquities of Selborne* published.

William Herschel built 12 m/40 ft telescope.

Mutiny on Captain Bligh's *HMS Bounty.*

*1790*          Third Mysore War.

French chemist Nicolas Leblanc developed a process for making sodium carbonate from sodium chloride (common salt).

English archaeologist John Frere identified Old Stone Age (Palaeolithic) tools together with large extinct animals.

*1791*          Canada divided into Upper and Lower Canada, and allowed representative government.

US Congress ratified Bill of Rights.

Slave rebellion on Haiti led by Pierre Toussaint L'Ouverture.

Neo-Classical architect Robert Adam designed Charlotte Square, Edinburgh.

*1792*          Gustaf III of Sweden assassinated.

Russian Empire extended to Black Sea.

British took Cape of Good Hope.

Italian physicist Alessandro Volta demonstrated the electrochemical series.

| | |
|---|---|
| *1793* | Execution of Louis XVI. |
| | Start of Revolutionary Wars between France and neighbouring states. |
| | Reign of Terror began in France, led by Maximilien Robespierre. |
| | Second partition of Poland: Russia and Prussia seized further areas. |
| | Cotton gin invented in USA, for mechanical separation of fibres from seeds. |
| | French naturalist Jean Baptiste de Lamarck argued that fossils are the remains of once living animals and plants. |
| *1794* | Slave trade in French colonies ended. |
| | Terror ended in France; rule by Directory began. |
| | British captured Corsica from French. |
| *1795* | Russia, Austria, and Prussia divided the remainder of Poland between them; Russia got Lithuania. |
| | In France, anatomist Georges Cuvier identified fossil bones of an extinct reptile. |
| | Composer and inventor Thomas Wright introduced metronome markings. |
| | The metric system was adopted in France. |
| | Scottish explorer Mungo Park began to trace course of Niger River. |
| *1796* | War broke out between Britain and Spain. |
| | Britain captured Guyana and Ceylon (Sri Lanka). |
| | Republic of Venice overthrown by Napoleon. |
| | In England, Edward Jenner established the |

practice of vaccination against smallpox, laying the foundations for theories of antibodies and immune reactions.

*1798*     French invaded Egypt.

Ceylon (Sri Lanka) became a British crown colony.

The link between heat and friction was discovered by British physicist Benjamin Rumford.

The *Allgemeine Musikalische Zeitung*, a journal of music criticism, was first published in Leipzig.

Norwegian mathematician Caspar Wessel introduced the vector representation of complex numbers.

English poets Wordsworth and Coleridge collaborated on Lyrical Ballads.

*1799*     Napoleon seized power as First Consul of France.

Kingdom of Mysore divided between Britain and Hyderabad.

Combination Act in UK outlawed elementary trade unions.

---

*Karl Friedrich Gauss of Germany proved the fundamental theorem of algebra: the number of solutions of an algebraic equation is the same as the exponent of the highest term.Advertisements contain the only truths to be relied upon in a newspaper.*
**Thomas Jefferson**

| | |
|---|---|
| *1800* | Thomas Jefferson became US president. |
| | Italian Alessandro Volta invented the voltaic cell. |
| *1801* | Act of Union (Britain and Ireland). |
| | French defeated Turks at Heliopolis, but later left Egypt. |
| | Battle of Copenhagen: British naval victory under Admiral Nelson over Danish fleet. |
| | Interference of light (the interaction of two or more waves) was discovered by British physicist Thomas Young. |
| | British engineer Richard Trevithick built a steam coach. |
| | French textile manufacturer Joseph Marie Jacquard developed an automatic loom controlled by punch cards. |
| | Giuseppe Piazzi in Palermo discovered the first asteroid, Ceres. |
| | German composer Ludwig van Beethoven's *Moonlight Sonata* completed. |
| *1802* | Peace of Amiens (Britain and France). |
| | Napoleon appointed First Consul for life. |
| | Scottish engineer William Symington launched the first stern paddle-wheel steamer, the *Charlotte Dundas*. |
| *1803* | Louisiana Purchase by USA of large tract of land from France. |
| | Britain and France at war again: Napoleonic Wars (until 1815). |
| | Second Maratha War in India. |
| *1804* | Napoleon became emperor of the French. |

Haiti independent from France.

Serbian uprisings against Turkish domination began.

Castle Hill rising of Irish convicts in New South Wales.

Lewis and Clark expedition in USA to find land route to Pacific. French physicists Jean Biot and Joseph Gay-Lussac studied the atmosphere from a hot-air balloon.

Richard Trevithick built the first steam locomotive and ran it on the track at the Pen-y-darren ironworks in South Wales.

**1805** Battle of Trafalgar, 21 Oct prevented French invasion of the UK.

---

*England expects every man will do his duty.*
**Horatio Nelson**
At the Battle of Trafalgar

---

Battle of Austerlitz: French victory over Austria and Russia.

Napoleon crowned himself king of Italy.

Albanian officer Mehemet Ali proclaimed pasha of Egypt.

Beethoven's *Eroica Symphony* vastly expanded the horizons of orchestral music.

**1806** Britain seized Cape Colony from Dutch.

Battle of Jena: French defeated Prussians.

Holy Roman Empire abolished; Napoleon united W Germany in the Confederation of the Rhine.

British admiral Francis Beaufort devised a scale

of wind strengths, the Beaufort Scale.

**1807**

Treaty of Tilsit: Russia changed sides in Napoleonic Wars and attacked Sweden.

British bombardment of Copenhagen caused Denmark to side with France.

Slave trade abolished by Britain.

Colombian independence movement started in Venezuela.

The first successful steamboat, the *Clermont*, designed by US engineer and inventor Robert Fulton, sailed between New York and Albany.

English chemist Humphry Davy passed electric current through molten compounds (the process of electrolysis) to isolate elements, such as potassium, that had never been separated by chemical means.

Swedish chemist Jöns Berzelius proposed that chemicals produced by living creatures should be termed 'organic'.

In France, Joseph Fourier showed that mathematical functions can be represented by trigonometric series.

**1808**

Peninsular War began with French invasion of Spain and Portugal; Britain sent expeditionary forces under Arthur Wellesley (the future Duke of Wellington).

The 'modern' atomic theory was propounded by British chemist John Dalton.

He also drew up a list of relative atomic masses.

Goethe completed his great philosophical verse drama *Faust*.

| | |
|---|---|
| *1809* | Ecuador became part of Colombia. |
| | Russia seized Finland, which became a grand duchy. |
| | Lamarck advocated a theory of evolution through inheritance of acquired characters. |
| *1810* | Spanish artist Francisco Goya began his series of etchings *The Disasters of War*, realistically depicting contemporary scenes of the Peninsular War. |
| *1811* | Luddite riots began in England against mechanization of production. |
| | Massacre of Mamelukes in the Middle East. |
| | Paraguay and Venezuela gained independence. |
| | Avogadro's hypothesis relating volumes and numbers of molecules of gases was proposed by Italian physicist Amedeo Avogadro. |
| | Jane Austen's novel *Sense and Sensibility* was published in England. |
| *1812* | Napoleon was forced to retreat from Russia by severe winter cold and scorched-earth defence tactics. |
| | Economic measures against Napoleonic France interfered with US trade and caused the War of 1812 between USA and UK. |
| | Chinese edict against Christianity. |
| | French astronomer and mathematician Pierre Simon Laplace published the first complete account of probability theory. |
| | The first two cantos of English poet Lord Byron's long narrative poem *Childe Harold* published. |

*Fair Greece! Sad Relic of departed worth!*
*Immortal, though no more; though fallen, great!*
**Byron** on Greece
*Childe Harold* 1812

*1813*      Quadruple Alliance between Austria, Britain,
           Prussia, and Russia to defeat Napoleon.

           Berzelius devised the chemical symbols and
           formulae still used to represent elements and
           compounds.

*1814*      Napoleon forced to abdicate and banished to
           Elba.

           Congress of Vienna to settle peace terms.

           Restoration of Bourbons in France.

           Norway independent of Denmark; ceded to
           Sweden.

           Treaty of Ghent ended war between Britain and
           USA.

           Cape Province sold to British.

           Dark lines in the solar spectrum were mapped by
           German physicist Joseph von Fraunhofer.

*1815*      Napoleon's Hundred Days: escaped from Elba.

*Had I succeeded, I should have died with the*
*reputation of the greatest man that ever lived.*
**Napoleon I**

Corn Law enacted in Britain by Lord
Liverpool's government.

Battle of Waterloo, 18 June: Napoleon defeated

by British forces under Wellington.

Napoleon abdicated in favour of his son; exiled to St Helena.

German Confederation of the Rhine formed.

Risorgimento movement for Italian national unity formed.

Norway awarded to Sweden by Congress of Vienna.

Austrian composer Franz Schubert's output for this year included two symphonies, two masses, 20 waltzes, and 145 songs.

In England, William Smith showed how rock strata (layers) can be identified on the basis of the fossils found in them.

**1816** United Provices of South American Argentine independent.

Shaka began to unite the Zulu clans in SE Africa.

**1817** Third Maratha War in India.

Ceylon (Sri Lanka) revolt suppressed by British.

John Keats's *Poems* published in England.

**1818** Chile independent.

French marshal Bernadotte, in Sweden from 1810, was made king of Sweden, the Vasa dynasty becoming extinct.

German philosopher Arthur Schopenhauer set out his pessimistic but influential world view in *The World as Will and Idea*.

English novelist Mary Shelley wrote seminal Gothic horror story *Frankenstein*.

**1819** Singapore founded as British colony.

Colombia independent.

USA bought Florida from Spain.

Peterloo massacre in England: cavalry charged demonstrators.

Antarctica was circumnavigated by Russian explorer Fabian von Bellingshausen.

The discovery of electromagnetism was made by Hans Oersted.

*1820*     Missouri Compromise: an agreement to admit Missouri, with slavery, and Maine, without it, to the USA at the same time.

Egypt conquered Sudan.

*1821*     Greek War of Independence from Turkey.

Mexico, Central America, and Peru proclaimed independence.

The dynamo principle was described by English physicist and chemist Michael Faraday.

The thermocouple was invented by German physicist Thomas Seebeck.

Carl von Weber's *Der Freischutz* introduced heroic German Romanticism to opera.

John Constable painted *The Hay Wain* in England.

*1822*     Brazil independent.

Liberia founded for freed slaves.

The laws of electrodynamics were established by French physicist André Ampère.

Mary Ann Mantell discovered on the English coast the first fossil to be recognized as that of a dinosaur (an iguanodon).

In Germany, Friedrich Mohs introduced a scale for specifying mineral hardness.

In the UK, Charles Babbage began construction of the first mechanical computer, the difference engine, a device for calculating logarithms and trigonometric functions.

Jean François Champollion deciphered Egyptian hieroglyphics.

English poet Percy Bysshe Shelley drowned in Italy.

**1823** Monroe Doctrine in US: President Monroe declared that any further colonial ambitions in the western hemisphere would be considered a threat to US peace; if left alone, USA would not interfere in European affairs.

British navigator James Weddell sailed into the Antarctic sea now named after him.

**1824** First Ashanti War: the British fought the Ashanti in Ghana for control of W African trade.

Peru independent.

General Chakri of Siam founded new dynasty.

Thermodynamics as a branch of physics was proposed by French scientist Sadi Carnot.

**1824–26** First Anglo-Burmese War: UK seized a coastal strip.

**1825** Bolivia independent.

Decembrist uprising in Russia against tsar.

George Stephenson in England built the first public railway to carry steam trains the Stockton and Darlington line using his engine *Locomotion*.

*Blessings on Science, and her handmaid Steam/*
*They make Utopia only half a dream.*
**Charles Mackay** on railways
*Railways* 1846

Cuvier proposed his theory of catastrophes as the cause of the extinction of large groups of animals.

**1826** Straits Settlements formed by East India Company.

UK gained control of Assam.

Sheikh Ahmadu conquered Timbuktu.

First Pan-American Congress in Panama.

French doctor Joseph Nicéphore Niepce produced the first photograph, with an exposure time of eight hours.

**1827** Battle of Navarino: Turkish and Egyptian fleets destroyed by English, French, and Russians in the war to liberate Greece.

John Walker invented phosphorus matches.

Ohm's law of electrical resistance was established by German physicist Georg Ohm.

Brownian motion resulting from molecular vibrations was observed by Scottish botanist Robert Brown.

**1828** Western Australia founded.

Uruguay independent.

Andrew Jackson elected US president.

The limits of instrumental virtuosity were redefined by Italian violinist Niccolò Paganini's

Vienna debut.

1829    Greece independent.

In Russia, Nikolai Ivanovich Lobachevsky developed hyperbolic geometry.

In France, mathematician Evariste Galois introduced the theory of groups.

The law of gaseous diffusion was established by Thomas Graham.

Stephenson designed his locomotive *Rocket*.

Scottish explorer John Ross discovered the magnetic North Pole.

The first success of French novelist Balzac: *La Physiologie du mariage/The Physiology of Marriage*.

---

1830    *Equality may perhaps be a right, but no power on Earth can turn it into a fact.*
**Honoré de Balzac**
*La Duchesse de Langeais*

---

Britain gained Mysore.

Russia conquered Kazakhstan.

Revolutions in France (Louis Philippe became king), Poland, Belgium, and Italy.

Partition of Gran Colombia.

Removal of American Indians to reservations began.

German anatomist Johannes Müller discovered proteins.

Scottish geologist Charles Lyell published the

first volume of *The Principles of Geology*, which described the Earth as being several hundred million years old.

Stephenson completed the Liverpool and Manchester Railway, the first steam passenger line.

French philosopher Auguste Comte coined the term 'sociology'.

Hector Berlioz's avant-garde and programmatic *Symphonie fantastique* startled Paris concert-goers.

Victor Hugo's verse play *Hernani* caused riots in Paris.

His work marked the beginning of a new Romantic drama, changing the course of French theatre.

**1830–48**    Algeria became a French colony after military conquest.

**1831**       Young Italy movement formed by Giuseppe Mazzini in exile in Marseille.

First nationalist revolt in Lithuania.

Grand opera was inaugurated with *Robert elle Diable* by German composer Giacomo Meyerbeer.

---

*Let me tell you that I – who am but a humble worm – am sometimes ill for a whole month after a first night.*
**Giacomo Meyerbeer**
Quoted in Harding Gounod

---

Electromagnetic induction was discovered by Faraday.

**1832**  Black Hawk War between US military and Sauk and Fox Indians.

Britain occupied Falkland Islands.

First Reform Act (Britain) shifted political power from upper to middle class.

Faraday expounded the laws of electrolysis, and adopted the term 'ion' for the particles believed to be responsible for carrying current.

Passenger trams came into use in New York.

**1833**  Prussian Zollverein formed; German customs union which also had the political effect of isolating Austria.

Anselme Payen and J F Persoz first isolated an enzyme.

**1834**  South Australia founded.

Slavery ended in British colonies.

Six farm labourers were transported to Australia for forming a trade union, but pardoned two years later; they were known as the Tolpuddle Martyrs after their Dorset village.

**1835**  Germany pioneered steam railways in Europe, using *Der Adler*, a locomotive built by Stephenson.

Tetrachloroethene (vinyl chloride) was first prepared.

In France, Joseph Niepce and Louis Daguerre produced the first daguerreotype photograph.

**1836**  Great Trek by Boers (Dutch settlers) to escape British rule in South Africa; they went on to found Transvaal and the Orange Free State.

Battles of the Alamo and San Jacinto: at the Alamo, a fortified mission in Texas, 180 Texans and US citizens held out for 11 days against 4,000 Mexicans led by Santa Anna.

Texas gained independence from Mexico.

The screw propeller was patented by Francis Pettit Smith in the UK.

Danish archaeologist Christian Thomsen devised the Stone, Bronze, and Iron Age classification.

Charles Dickens published the first number of *The Pickwick Papers*.

**1837**          Accession of Victoria as queen of the UK.

Colonization of New Zealand began.

Papineau and Mackenzie rebellions in Upper and Lower Canada.

Uprising in Osaka, Japan, prompted by famine and restrictive laws.

**1838**          Massacre of Zulus at Battle of Blood River.

Durham Report led to the union of Upper and Lower Canada.

British engineer Isambard Kingdom Brunel's *Great Western*, the first steamship built for crossing the Atlantic, sailed from Bristol to New York in 15 days.

J M W Turner in England painted *The Fighting Téméraire*; his free, luminous style anticipated Impressionism.

**1838–42**      First Afghan War: British garrison at Kabul wiped out.

| | |
|---|---|
| **1839** | Central America split into numerous states. |
| | First Chartist petition (of British democratic movement). |

---

*Political power our means, social happiness our end.*
**Slogan of Chartism**

---

| | |
|---|---|
| | Mehemet Ali, pasha of Egypt, defeated Ottomans. |
| | Theodor Schwann proposed that all living matter is made up of cells. |
| | Kirkpatrick Macmillan designed first treadle-powered bicycle. |
| **1839–42** | First Opium War: Britain forced China to accept opium in exchange for tea and to open five treaty ports. |
| **1840** | Treaty of Waitangi: Britain annexed New Zealand. |
| | Act of Union for Canada. |
| | Said ibn Sayyid took over Zanzibar. |
| | Matabeleland founded. |
| | Natal proclaimed. |
| | British archaeologist Austen Layard began excavating the Assyrian capital of Nineveh. |
| | In the USA, palaeontologist Louis Agassiz established that there had been ice ages in the past. |
| **1841** | Mehemet Ali recognized as hereditary ruler of Egypt, virtually independent of Ottomans. |

Britain occupied Hong Kong.

In Antarctica, Scottish explorer James Ross sighted the Great Ice Barrier now named after him.

Oregon Trail opened up: the first wagon trains of settlers left Missouri for California.

**1842** French occupied Tahiti.

Massacre at Khyber Pass during British retreat from Afghanistan.

Webster–Ashburton Treaty fixed the Maine–Canada border.

The Vienna Philharmonic Orchestra gave its first concerts.

English palaeontologist Richard Owen coined the name dinosaur for the reptiles, now extinct, that lived between about 200 and 65 million years ago.

The principle of conservation of energy was observed by Julius von Mayer.

**1843** French occupied Tahiti.

Britain conquered Sind.

Natal became a British colony.

Parliamentary government introduced in Greece after rebellion.

Samuel Morse transmitted the first message along a telegraph line in USA.

**1844** French mathematician Joseph Liouville found the first transcendental number, which cannot be expressed as an algebraic equation with rational coefficients.

In Germany, Hermann Grassmann studied

vectors with more than three dimensions.

**1845** Texas annexed by USA.

The first clipper ship, *Rainbow*, was launched in the USA.

*Great Britain*, built by Isambard Kingdom Brunel, became the first propeller-driven iron ship to cross the Atlantic.

**1845–46** Irish potato famine: 1.5 million people emigrated.

**1845–47** Maori revolt against colonists in New Zealand.

**1846** Corn Laws repealed in Britain.

Oregon Treaty settled boundary between USA and British possessions at the 49th parallel, dipping to keep Vancouver Island British.

Xhosa War against British and Dutch colonists in South Africa.

Irish physicist William Thomson (Lord Kelvin) estimated, using the temperature of the Earth, that the Earth is 100 million years old.

Scottish chemist Thomas Graham expounded his law of diffusion of gases and liquids.

The planet Neptune was located by Johann Galle, following predictions by John Adams and Urbain Leverrier.

**1846–48** Mexican-American War resulted in US territorial expansion.

**1847** Liberia independent.

The mechanical equivalent of heat was described by James Joule.

*Jane Eyre* by Charlotte Brontë and *Wuthering Heights* by her sister Emily were published in England.

**1848**  Short-lived republican revolutions throughout Europe.

French Second Republic established.

Communist Manifesto by Karl Marx and Friedrich Engels published.

Maya Indian revolt in Mexico suppressed.

Pre-Raphaelite Brotherhood of painters formed in England.

---

*A spectre is haunting Europe – the spectre of communism.*
**Karl Marx**
*The Communist Manifesto* 1848

---

**1849**  Main Californian Gold Rush took place.

Britain annexed Punjab after Sikh Wars.

**1850**  California joined USA.

Britain bought Danish settlements in W Africa.

Taiping Rebellion in China that undermined the Qing dynasty: the rebels instituted radical, populist reforms; civil war continued until 1864.

Victoria, Australia, separated from New South Wales.

US naval officer Matthew Fontaine Maury mapped the Atlantic Ocean, noting that it is deeper near its edges than at the centre.

Alfred, Lord Tennyson, was made poet laureate.

**1851**  British occupied Lagos.

Cuba unsuccessfully declared independence.

The rotation of the Earth was demonstrated by French physicist Jean Foucault.

US novelist Hern .1 Melville published *Moby Dick.*

International trade fair, the Great Exhibition, held in London. It was the brainchild of Albert, Prince Consort of Queen Victoria.

---

*You Gentlemen of England . . .. can have little idea from reading the newspapers of the Horror and Misery of operating on these dying exhausted men.*
**Florence Nightingale**
Letter from Scutari 1854, during the Crimean War.

---

| | |
|---|---|
| *1852* | Fall of Second Republic in France: Napoleon III took power. |
| | Second Burmese War: Britain annexed Lower Burma, including Rangoon (Yangon). |
| | French inventor Henri Giffard flew the first steam-powered airship over Paris. |
| | Edward Sabine in Ireland showed a link between sunspot activity and changes in the Earth's magnetic field. |
| *1853* | Russo-Turkish war over Palestine. |
| | Britain annexed Nagpur in Maharashtra, India. |
| | George Cayley in the UK flew the first true aeroplane, a model glider 1.5 m/5 ft long. |
| *1853–54* | Gadsden Purchase: US acquisition of |

Mexican territory.

USA forced Japan to resume international relations and trade.

**1853–56**    Crimean War (Britain, France, Turkey, and Sardinia against Russia). It saw the introduction of war photography and professional nursing.

**1854**       Elgin Treaty over Canadian trade by USA and Britain.

George Boole in the UK published his system of symbolic logic, now called Boolean algebra.

In Weimar, Germany, Hungarian pianist Franz Liszt conducted the premières of his first symphonic poems.

---

*To us musicians the work of Beethoven parallels the pillars of smoke and fire which led the Israelites through the desert.*
**Franz Liszt**
Letter to Wilhelm von Lenz 1852

---

**1855**       Treaty of Peshawar (Afghanistan and Britain).

Santa Anna overthrown in Mexico; liberal reforms introduced.

German chemist Robert von Bunsen invented the Bunsen burner.

The first technique was patented for the production of artificial fibres, from cellulose nitrate (nitrocellulose).

Death of Danish philosopher Søren Kierkegaard, founder of existentialism.

US poet Walt Whitman published the first

version of his *Leaves of Grass*.

**1856**        Britain annexed the kingdom of Oudh in N India.

Tasmania became self-governing.

Natal became a crown colony.

Persia at war with Britain after taking Herat in Afghanistan.

Henry Bessemer in the UK developed the first cheap method of making steel.

William Henry Perkin set up the first synthetic-dye factory, for the production of mauveine.

By establishing that micro-organisms are responsible for fermentation, French chemist Louis Pasteur created the discipline of microbiology.

**1857**        *Madame Bovary* by French novelist Gustave Flaubert published in France.

**1857–58**     Indian Mutiny of local soldiers against the British Raj, leading in places to a general uprising.

This was suppressed, and the British crown took over the government of India from the East India Company.

**1857–82**     Married Women's Property Acts passed in Britain: their belongings were no longer legally their husbands'.

**1858**        Treaty of Aigun: Russia gained Amur from China.

Vietnam conquered by France.

First transatlantic telegraph cable laid.

English mathematician Arthur Cayley developed

calculations using ordered tables called matrices.

Italian chemist Stanislao Cannizzaro differentiated between atomic and molecular weights (masses).

**1859**  France and Sardinia at war with Austria; Austrians expelled from Lombardy.

Morocco and Spain at war.

Charles Darwin published *On the Origin of Species*, expounding his theory of evolution by natural selection.

---

*What can be more curious than that the hand of a man formed for grasping, that of a mole for digging, [...] and the wing of a bat, should all be constructed on the same pattern, and should include the same bones, in the same relative positions?*
**Charles Darwin**
*On the Origin of Species*

---

English philosopher John Stuart Mill published the classic defence of liberalism, *On Liberty*.

Spectrographic analysis was made in Germany by Robert von Bunsen and Gustav Kirchhoff.

Edwin Drake drilled the world's first oil well at Titusville, Pennsylvania, USA.

Edward Fitzgerald's translation of *The Rubaiyat of Omar Khayyam* from Persian.

**1860**  End of Opium War: Britain and France occupied Beijing.

Confederacy formed by southern states of America.

Giuseppe Garibaldi won Naples and Sicily for the projected new kingdom of Italy.

Jean Etienne Lenoir built a gas-fuelled internal-combustion engine.

*1860–72*   Maori revolt in New Zealand.

*1861*   Lagos ceded to Britain.

American Civil War began.

Emancipation of Russian serfs.

Victor Emmanuel II proclaimed king of Italy.

Organic chemistry was defined by German chemist Friedrich Kekulé von Stradonitz as the chemistry of carbon compounds.

Belgian chemist Ernest Solvay patented a method for the production of sodium carbonate from sodium chloride and ammonia; the first production plant was established 1863.

The process of osmosis was discovered.

*1862*   Otto von Bismarck became prime minister of Prussia.

Prince Otto of Bavaria deposed from Greek throne and replaced by Prince George of Denmark.

Alexander Parkes produced the first known synthetic plastic (Parkesine, or xylonite) from cellulose nitrate, vegetable oils, and camphor; it was the forerunner of celluloid.

Haemoglobin was first crystallized.

Machine gun invented by Richard Gatling and used against American Indians.

Russian writer Ivan Turgenev's novel *Fathers and Sons* published.

Victor Hugo's novel *Les Misérables* dramatically highlighted social problems in France.

**1863**   Cambodia became a French protectorate.

Slavery abolished in USA and in Dutch colonies.

France occupied Mexico.

The explosive TNT discovered by German chemist J Wilbrand.

Edouard Manet's painting *Déjeuner sur l'herbe/ Picnic on the Grass* caused a scandal when first shown in Paris.

Russian novelist Leo Tolstoy began writing *War and Peace*.

Football Association founded in UK.

**1864**   Denmark and France at war with Prussian alliance; Denmark lost Schleswig-Holstein.

Triple Alliance (Paraguayan) War.

In the American Civil War, Union general Sherman marched through Georgia, taking Atlanta.

Maximilian of house of Habsburg made emperor of Mexico.

William Siemens and Pierre Emile Martin developed the Siemens-Martin process (open-hearth method) for the production of steel.

**1865**   Surrender of Confederate forces.

US President Abraham Lincoln assassinated by John Wilkes Booth.

*Tell mother – tell mother – I died for my country.*
**John Wilkes Booth**

Rebellion in Jamaica.

Lewis Carroll's classic children's story *Alice's Adventures in Wonderland* published in the UK.

German composer Richard Wagner's opera *Tristan und Isolde* scaled new heights of expressiveness using unprecedented chromaticism.

Schubert's *Unfinished Symphony* (1822) was premiered in Vienna.

*1866*  Austro-Prussian War.

Crete revolted against Turks.

Austrian biologist Gregor Mendel pioneered the study of inheritance with his experiments on peas, but achieved little recognition.

Russian novelist Fyodor Dostoevsky's *Crime and Punishment* published.

*Without God, all things are possible.*
**Fyodor Dostoevsky**

*1867*  Second Great Reform Act in Britain further extended the franchise.

Garibaldi's march on Rome.

The North German Confederation was formed, under the leadership of Prussia.

Meiji Restoration in Japan: executive power awarded to emperor; shogunate abolished.

Convict transportation to Australia ended.

Alaska purchased by USA from Russia.

Dominion of Canada established.

---

*I cannot offer you either wages or honours; I offer you hunger, thirst, forced marches, battles, and death. Anyone who loves his country, follow me.*
**Giuseppe Garibaldi**

---

French left Mexico; Emperor Maximilian executed.

Dynamite patented by Alfred Nobel.

The first volume of Karl Marx's *Das Kapital* was published.

With *The Fortune of the Rougons* Emile Zola began his series of novels portraying the fortunes of a French family.

Queensberry Rules of boxing drawn up in UK.

**1868**    Military rising in Spain.

Basutoland (now Lesotho) became a British protectorate.

Ku Klux Klan racist vigilante group formed in USA.

Cuba and Spain at war.

First Trades Union Congress held in UK.

**1869**    Suez Canal opened.

Italian colonial expansion began in NE Africa.

Red River Rebellion broke out in Canada.

German Social Democratic Workers' Party

founded. As Sozialdemokratische Partei from 1875, it was the first party to advocate gradual evolution of democratic socialism within existing political structures.

Dmitri Mendeleyev expounded his periodic table of the elements (based on atomic weight), leaving gaps for elements that had not yet been discovered.

The genetic material DNA (deoxyribonucleic acid) was discovered by Friedrich Mieschler.

The first US transcontinental railway was completed at Promontory, Utah, when the Union Pacific and the Central Pacific railroads met.

Celluloid was first produced from cellulose nitrate and camphor.

**1870**      Third Republic in France.

Franco-Prussian War.

Italy annexed Rome, completing Italian unification.

French composer Léo Delibes' ballet *Coppélia* presented in Paris.

**1871**      The Paris Commune, the world's first socialist government, held power March–May, until put down by force.

German Empire formed under William I of Prussia with Bismarck as chancellor.

British Columbia and Vancouver joined Dominion of Canada.

Britain annexed Kimberley diamond fields in South Africa.

Military conflict between settlers and Apaches in

North America.

Heinrich Schliemann began excavations at Troy.

The first part of George Eliot's novel *Middlemarch* published in UK.

Rugby Football Union formed in England.

**1872**      Russian anarchist Mikhail Bakunin expelled from the First International (coordinating socialist body) by Karl Marx.

Albert Memorial in London completed to a design by Gilbert Scott, the leading Gothic revival architect.

First annual FA Cup football competition held in England and Wales.

**1873**      Second Ashanti War of British conquest in W Africa.

Light was conceived as electromagnetic radiation by Scottish physicist James Maxwell.

**1874**      Britain annexed Fiji.

Gold Coast (Ghana) colony founded by Britain.

Thomas Hardy's novel *Far From the Madding Crowd* was his first success in the UK.

First Impressionist art exhibition held in Paris.

American football invented at Harvard University.

**1875**      The first of a series of collaborations between composer Arthur Sullivan and librettist W S Gilbert, the operetta *Trial by Jury*, was given its premiere in the UK.

**1876**      Battle of Little Big Horn; Sioux and Cheyenne Indians led by Sitting Bull and Crazy Horse destroyed General Custer's cavalry.

Korea independent.

Turks massacred Bulgarians.

Wagner's opera sequence *Der Ring des Nibelungen/The Ring of the Nibelung* was produced in Bayreuth.

German composer Johannes Brahms's *First Symphony* was performed.

---

*It is not hard to compose, but it is wonderfully hard to let the superfluous notes fall under the table.*
**Johannes Brahms**

---

Nikolaus August Otto introduced the four-stroke cycle used in the modern internal-combustion engine.

Scottish scientist Alexander Graham Bell patented his invention, the telephone.

---

*Mr Watson, come here; I want you.*
**Alexander Graham Bell**
*First words spoken over the telephone 7 March 1876*

---

English cricketer W G Grace scored the first triple century.

*1877*    Queen Victoria became empress of India.

Satsuma rebellion in Japan: samurai uprising suppressed by newly formed imperial army.

Britain annexed Transvaal and Orange Free State.

Last Xhosa war in southern Africa.

A theory of sound as vibrations in an elastic medium was propounded by British physicist John Rayleigh.

US inventor Thomas Alva Edison invented the cylindrical tin-foil phonograph, but few showed interest.

The ballet *Swan Lake* with music by Tchaikovsky, premiered in Moscow, was a failure through poor production and choreography.

First cricket test match played in Melbourne by Australian and English teams.

First tennis championship held at Wimbledon, S London.

| | |
|---|---|
| **1877–78** | Russo-Turkish War. |
| **1878** | Congress of Berlin: European powers redrew boundaries in the Balkans. |

Serbia became an independent kingdom after liberation war against Turks.

Second Afghan War: UK seized Kabul.

Stone Age paintings were first discovered at Altamira, Spain.

English scientist William Crookes invented a vacuum tube that produces cathode rays.

**1879**     Treaty of San Stefano (Russia and Turkey).

Dual Alliance (Austria and Germany).

Zulu Wars with British and Boers broke out in South Africa.

Britain and France took control of Egypt.

War of the Pacific: Chile defeated Peru and

Bolivia, which lost its coastline.

Edison invented the electric light bulb.

Photogravure process invented.

Ernst Werner von Siemens demonstrated an electric train in Germany.

Henrik Ibsen's *A Doll's House*, an early example of realism in European theatre, published in Copenhagen.

*1880*        French annexed Tahiti.

Piezoelectric effect was discovered by French scientist Pierre Curie.

Augustus Pitt-Rivers developed the concept of stratigraphy in archaeology.

*1881*        First South African War between Boers and British.

First pogroms against Jews in Russia and Poland.

French invaded Tunis.

Nationalist revolt in Egypt against French.

Nationalist revolt began in Sudan against Egypt.

*1882*        Triple Alliance (Italy, Germany, and Austria) formed.

French left Egypt to British, who occupied Cairo.

French captured Hanoi, Vietnam.

German bacteriologist Robert Koch isolated the bacillus responsible for tuberculosis.

*1883*        Metropolitan Opera House opened in New York with a production of Charles Gounod's *Faust*.

France presented Frédéric Bartholdi's enormous

Statue of Liberty to USA.

Spanish architect Antonio Gaudí began the Art Nouveau Neo-Gothic Sagrada Familia/Church of the Holy Family in Barcelona.

French painter Claude Monet settled at Giverny. The garden and lily pond he constructed there were to inspire many of his paintings.

Publication began of German philosopher Friedrich Nietzsche's *Also sprach Zarathustra/ Thus Spoke Zarathustra*. His rejection of Christianity as a slave morality and his concept of the 'superman' proved influential.

*1884*     Berlin Conference accelerated European scramble for Africa: Belgium, France, Germany, Portugal, and the UK divided up the continent between them.

Germany acquired SW Africa, and in W Africa Togoland and Cameroon.

Annam became part of French Indochina.

Edwin Klebs isolated the diphtheria bacillus.

Swedish chemist Svante Arrhenius suggested that electrolytes (solutions or molten compounds that conduct electricity) dissociate into ions, atoms, or groups of atoms that carry a positive or negative charge.

Hiram Maxim invented automatic machine gun.

US author Mark Twain published *The Adventures of Huckleberry Finn*, a picaresque novel.

French sculptor Auguste Rodin began *Les Bourgeois de Calais/The Burghers of Calais*, a realistic bronze group.

**1885**    Germany annexed Tanganyika and Zanzibar.

Anglo-Burmese War: Britain annexed Upper Burma, and rest joined India.

Leopold II of Belgium established the Congo Free State (now Zaire), from where he soon extracted a fortune by ruthless exploitation.

British garrison at Khartoum, Sudan, fell to nationalist rebels after long siege.

The trans-Canada continental railway was completed, from Montréal in the east to Port Moody, British Columbia, in the west.

Indian National Congress formed, leading the movement against British rule.

Liszt composed *Bagatelle without Tonality* (his *Faust Symphony* of 1857 opened with a 12-note row).

In Germany, Gottlieb Daimler developed a successful lightweight petrol engine and fitted it to a bicycle to create a prototype motorcycle; Karl Benz fitted his lightweight petrol engine to a three-wheeled carriage to pioneer the motorcar.

Louis Pasteur produced a vaccine against rabies.

**1886**    Spain ended slavery in Cuba.

Royal Niger Company formed; Lagos became a British colony.

German engineer Gottlieb Daimler built the first boat powered by an internal-combustion engine and fitted his engine to a four-wheeled carriage to produce a four-wheeled motorcar.

Linotype machine for hot-metal typesetting

invented by Ottmar Mergenthaler in USA.

French artist Georges Seurat painted the Neo-Impressionist *Sunday on the Island of La Grande Jatte*.

**1887** The existence of radio waves was predicted by German physicist Heinrich Hertz.

Italian composer Giuseppe Verdi wrote the opera *Otello*.

**1888** Slavery ended in Brazil.

August Strindberg wrote *Miss Julie*.

---

*I see the playwright as a lay preacher peddling the ideas of his time in popular form.*
**August Strindberg**
Preface to *Miss Julie* 1888

---

William Friese-Greene showed the first celluloid film and patented a moving-picture camera.

Dutch Post-Impressionist Vincent van Gogh cut off his ear after a quarrel with fellow painter Paul Gauguin.

**1889** Italy gained control of Eritrea.

Abyssinia (Ethiopia) reunited under Menelik II.

London dock strike.

Brazil a republic.

Edward Barnard took the first photographs of the Milky Way.

Gustave Eiffel built iron tower as temporary structure for Paris exhibition.

**1890** Rhodesia formed.

Britain annexed Uganda.

Zanzibar settlement (Britain took it over from Germany).

Battle of Wounded Knee, the last major battle between American Indians and US troops.

William James in USA published the first comprehensive psychology text, *Principles of Psychology.*

Joseph Lister demonstrated antiseptic surgery in UK.

English geologist Arthur Holmes used radioactivity to date rocks, establishing the Earth to be 4.6 billion years old.

The first electric underground railway opened in London.

*1891* German aviator Otto Lilienthal piloted a glider in flight.

Flinders Petrie began excavating Akhetaton in Egypt.

Rayon was invented.

*1892* The first automatic telephone exchange was opened in USA.

German mathematician Georg Cantor showed that there are different kinds of infinity and studied transfinite numbers.

*1893* Hawaiian monarchy overthrown.

Laos became part of French Indochina.

Matabeleland (now W Zimbabwe) occupied by Britain.

France gained Ivory Coast.

Norwegian explorer Fridtjof Nansen proved that

no Arctic continent existed when his ship drifted across the Arctic while locked in ice.

Women's right to vote pioneered by New Zealand.

Norwegian Edvard Munch produced the symbolic Expressionist painting *Skriket/The Scream.*

Irish dramatist George Bernard Shaw wrote *Mrs Warren's Profession* (banned until 1902 because it deals with prostitution).

---

*I accuse.*
**Émile Zola**
*Open letter to the French president 1898 condemning the French army's treatment of Captain Dreyfus*

---

**1894**    Dreyfus affair began in France: army officer Alfred Dreyfus was court-martialled on false charges as a result of anti-Semitism, and sent to Devil's Island penal colony. A retrial 1899 again found him guilty, and he was not exonerated until 1906 after a public outcry.

Guomindang Chinese National People's Party founded by Sun Yat-sen.

In the UK, William Ramsey and Lord Rayleigh discovered the first inert (or noble) gas, argon.

**1894–95**    First Sino-Japanese War (over Korea).

**1895**    Cuba rebelled against Spain.

X-rays were discovered by German physicist Wilhelm Röntgen.

Sigmund Freud's first book on psychoanalysis was published in Austria.

In the USA, Jeanette Picard launched the first balloon to be used for stratospheric research.

Oscar Wilde's comedy *The Importance of Being Earnest* was the Irish writer's greatest success; later the same year he was imprisoned for homosexual acts.

The French Lumière brothers projected, to a paying audience, a film of an oncoming train.

Alfred Jarry's play *Ubu Roi* was a forerunner of Surrealism in France.

French mathematician Jules Henri Poincaré published the first paper on topology, often called 'the geometry of rubber sheets'.

---

*Science is built up with facts, as a house is with stones. But a collection of facts is no more a science than a heap of stones is a house.*
**Jules Henri Poincaré**
*La Science et l' hypothèse* 1902

---

**1896**

French annexed Madagascar.

Britain won last Ashanti War.

Italian invasion of Abyssinia (Ethiopia) defeated.

Zionist movement for a Jewish homeland in Palestine founded by Theodor Herzl.

Anglo-Egyptian army under Lord Kitchener confronted Sudanese rebellion.

The discovery of radioactivity was made by

French physicist Antoine Becquerel.

Scottish Art Nouveau architect Charles Rennie Mackintosh designed the Glasgow School of Art.

The first performance of Russian writer Anton Chekhov's play *The Seagull* failed.

The first Olympic Games in modern times were held in Athens.

**1897**      Greece and Turkey at war over Crete.

Martinus Beijerinck discovered viruses.

English physicist J J Thomson discovered the electron.

**1898**      Fashoda Incident: clash between British and French forces in SE Sudan.

Britain agreed 99-year lease from China of New Territories (Hong Kong).

Spanish-American War: Spain lost Cuba, the Philippines, and Puerto Rico.

USA annexed Hawaii.

English writer H G Wells published the science-fiction novel *The War of the Worlds*.

**1899**      Second South African War.

British forces set up the first concentration camps, for Afrikaner civilians.

Sudan became an Anglo-Egyptian condominium.

New Zealand physicist Ernest Rutherford discovered alpha and beta rays.

Felix Hoffman developed aspirin.

English archaeologist Arthur Evans began to excavate Minoan Knossos in Crete.

**1900**        North and South Nigeria became British protectorates.

In war with Boers, strongholds of Ladysmith, Kimberley, and Mafeking relieved by British forces under Sir Redvers Buller.

Britain annexed Orange Free State and Transvaal.

First Pan-African Conference.

Boxer Rebellion in Beijing against Europeans and Chinese Christians.

Labour Party founded in UK.

Austrian immunologist Karl Landsteiner identified three blood groups, later designated A, B, and O.

Mendel's work was rediscovered and the science of genetics founded.

Quantum theory was framed by German physicist Max Planck.

The discovery of gamma rays was made by French physicist Paul-Ulrich Villard.

---

*A new scientific truth does not triumph by convincing its opponents ...but rather because its opponents eventually die, and a new generation grows up that is familiar with it.*
**Max Planck**
*Autobiography* 1949

---

Joseph Conrad's novel *Lord Jim* published in UK.

Davis Cup for tennis first contested.

**1901**            Australian Commonwealth established.

Cuba became nominally independent, though with strong US presence.

Philippine nationalist revolt, which began 1898, suppressed by USA (having killed one-fifth of population).

Russia occupied Manchuria.

Queen Victoria died; succeeded by Edward VII.

English explorer Robert Scott first penetrated the interior of the Antarctic.

Italian electrical engineer Guglielmo Marconi transmitted the first radio signals across the Atlantic.

Okapi discovered in Africa.

**1902**            End of South African War.

Anglo-German force seized Venezuelan fleet.

Russian revolutionaries Leon Trotsky and V I Lenin first met, in exile.

British physicist Oliver Heaviside discovered the ionosphere.

Premiere of opera *Pelléas et Mélisande* by French composer Claude Debussy.

**1903**            First powered and controlled flight of a heavier-than-air craft (aeroplane) by Orville Wright, at Kitty Hawk, North Carolina, USA.

Russian scientist Konstantin Tsiolkovsky published the first practical paper on aeronautics.

Russian physiologist Ivan Pavlov reported his early study on conditioned reflexes in animals.

Russian Social Democratic Party split into

Bolsheviks and Mensheviks.

The first Western film was made in the USA.

*1904*      Entente Cordiale (Britain and France).

Germans massacred Herero rebels, S W Africa.

Treaty between Bolivia and Chile.

The theory of radioactivity was put forward by Rutherford and Frederick Soddy.

Polish scientist Marie Curie discovered radioactive elements radium and polonium.

John Fleming invented the thermionic valve (electron tube) in UK.

*1904–05*   Russo-Japanese War: Japan successfully besieged Port Arthur and destroyed the Russian Baltic fleet in Tsushima Strait.

Russia ceded S Sakhalin to Japan and evacuated Manchuria.

---

*What this country needs is a short victorious war to stem the tide of revolution.*
**Vyacheslav Plehve**
Shortly before the Russo-Japanese War

---

*1905*      Revolution in Russia; first soviet (local workers' council) set up in St Petersburg.

New constitution provided for assembly.

Norway independent from Sweden.

German-born physicist Albert Einstein published his special theory of relativity.

*1906*      Algeciras Conference: international summit meeting to apportion control of Morocco (it was given to France and Spain).

Militant suffragette campaign launched in UK by Emmeline Pankhurst and her daughters.

Earthquake in San Francisco devasted city and killed 3,000 people.

Russian dancer and choreographer Vaslav Nijinsky made his debut.

**1907**          Triple Entente (France, Britain, and Russia).

New Zealand an independent dominion.

Dutch conquered Sumatra.

Spanish artist Pablo Picasso completed *Les Demoiselles d'Avignon*, a painting that inspired Cubism.

**1908**          Bulgaria independent.

Young Turk Revolution by army officers in Ottoman Empire brought about constitutional changes.

Belgium took over Congo Free State from the personal control of Leopold II.

Bosnian crisis: Austria annexed Bosnia and Herzegovina from Turkey.

Fragment of comet fell at Tunguska, Siberia.

Dutch took over Bali.

Muslim League formed.

Fritz Haber invented the Haber process for the production of ammonia from nitrogen and hydrogen.

First powered flight in the UK by Samuel Cody.

The Geiger counter for measuring nuclear radiation was invented by German physicist

Hans Geiger and Ernest Rutherford.

In the USA, Henry Ford's Model T was the first car to be built solely by mass-production methods.

---

*History is more or less bunk. The only history that is worth a tinker's dam is the history we make today.*
**Henry Ford**

---

*1909*

Louis Blériot flew across the English Channel from France to England by plane in 36 minutes.

The first totally synthetic plastic (Bakelite) was produced by Leo Baekeland.

US explorer Robert E Peary became first person to reach North Pole.

*Futurist Manifesto* published by Italian poet Filippo Marinetti.

A new style to glorify the machine age was created in painting (Giacomo Balla), sculpture (Umberto Boccioni), and music (Georges Antheil), but Futurism did not outlast World War I.

| | |
|---|---|
| *1910* | Revolution in Mexico: capitalist dictator Porfirio Diaz overthrown. |
| | Revolution in Portugal: republic proclaimed. |
| | Revolution in Iran (following an earlier one in 1905) led to the establishment of parliamentary government. |
| | South Africa became independent dominion. |
| | Japan annexed Korea. |
| | China ended slavery. |
| | Paul Ehrlich developed the first specific antibacterial agent, Salvarsan, a cure for syphilis. |
| | In Vienna, Austrian Adolf Loos designed the *Steiner House*, a very early example of modern architecture. |
| *1911* | Agadir incident: international crisis provoked by Germany in Morocco. |
| | Italy conquered Libya. |
| | Revolution in China, led by Sun Yat-sen: republic established. |
| | The ruined Inca city of Machu Pichu was discovered by Hiram Bingham in the Andes. |
| | Norwegian explorer Roald Amundsen reached the South Pole, 14 Dec, overland with dogs. |
| | The discovery of the atomic nucleus was made by Ernest Rutherford. |
| *1911–12* | Italy and Turkey at war. |
| *1912* | Arizona and New Mexico joined USA. |
| | African National Congress founded to extend franchise to whole population of South Africa. |

In Germany, Alfred Wegener proposed the theory of continental drift and the existence of a supercontinent, Pangaea, in the distant past.

'Unsinkable' passenger liner *Titanic* struck an iceberg off Grand Banks of Newfoundland and sank on its first voyage.

The first diesel locomotive took to the rails in Germany.

Austro-Hungarian composer Arnold Schoenberg's atonal *Pierrot Lunaire*, for reciter and chamber ensemble, foreshadowed many similar small-scale quasi-theatrical works.

English explorer Robert Falcon Scott reached the South Pole, 18 Jan, initially aided by ponies.

Swiss painter Paul Klee and Wassily Kandinsky, Russian pioneer of abstract art, were members of the Blaue Reiter group of artists in Munich.

*1912–13*  Balkan Wars resulted in the expulsion of Ottoman Turkey from the Balkan states.

*1913*  The orbiting electron atomic theory was put forward by Danish physicist Niels Bohr.

Henry Moseley equated the atomic number of an element with the positive charge on its nuclei, and drew up the periodic table, based on atomic number, that is used today.

Igor Stravinsky's ballet *The Rite of Spring* precipitated a riot at its premiere in Paris.

French artist Marcel Duchamp exhibited an upturned bicycle wheel, first of a series of 'ready-mades'.

English novelist D H Lawrence's *Sons and Lovers* published.

*I like to write when I feel spiteful; it's like having
a good sneeze.*
**D H Lawrence**
Letter to Lady Cynthia Asquith Nov 1913

*1914*

Assassination of the heir to the Austrian throne
(28 June) triggered the start of World War I
between Central Powers (Germany,
Austria-Hungary, and allies) and the Triple
Entente (UK and the British Empire, France,
Russia, and allies); Britain entered the war 4
Aug.

Battle of Tannenberg: Germans under
Hindenburg defeated Russians.

Egypt and Cyprus declared British protectorates.

Panama Canal opened.

*It is the greatest liberty that Man has ever taken
with Nature.*
**James Bryce**
On the Panama Canal, South America 1912

Nigeria united to form Britain's largest African
colony.

*1915*

Italy joined Allies.

Bulgaria joined Central Powers.

Mahatma Gandhi returned to India to lead the
nonviolent resistance to British rule.

Poison gas (chlorine) used in warfare for the first
time, by the Germans.

**1915–16**      Gallipoli campaign: unsuccessful attempt by mainly Australian and New Zealand troops to cross the Dardanelles strait to Turkey.

*If I should die think only this of me:/ That there's some corner of a foreign field/ That is forever England.*
**Rupert Brooke**
*The Soldier* 1915

Dada anarchic avant-garde movement in the arts founded in Zurich, Switzerland.

D W Griffith's epic film *The Birth of a Nation* released in USA.

**1916**      Battles of Verdun, Jutland, and the Somme.

Portugal and Romania joined war against Germany.

Easter Rising in Ireland, suppressed by British army.

Haile Selassie became regent of Ethiopia.

US bought Danish West Indies (Virgin Islands).

Albert Einstein put forward his general theory of relativity.

**1917**      USA declared war on Germany, Hungary, and Austria.

USA bought Dutch West Indies.

Revolutions in Russia.

Tsar Nicholas II abdicated in March; in Oct, the Bolsheviks seized power from the provisional government.

Balfour Declaration promised the Jews a

homeland in Palestine.

Anglo-US writer T S Eliot's first volume of poetry, *Prufrock and Other Observations*, published.

Design magazine *De Stijl* cofounded by Dutch painter Piet Mondrian.

*1918*    Britain captured Syria.

Central Powers surrendered.

Armistice signed 11 Nov.

Weimar Republic established in Germany.

Kingdom created in Balkans that united Serbia, Croatia, Slovenia, and Montenegro (named Yugoslavia from 1921).

*1918–22*   Civil war in Russia between Red (revolutionary) and White (reactionary) forces.

*1919*    Third Afghan War: Afghanistan achieved full independence.

Amritsar Massacre: British troops fired on demonstrators in India.

Treaty of Versailles: peace agreement between the Allies and Germany.

Germany suffered territorial losses and other restrictions.

Irish Republican Army (IRA) formed; guerrilla warfare against British troops.

Democratic republic established in Lithuania.

Elwood Haynes patented stainless steel.

First E–W flight across the Atlantic by Albert C Read, using a flying boat; first non-stop flight across the Atlantic E–W by John William Alcock and Arthur Whitten Brown in 16 hours

27 minutes; first complete flight from Britain to Australia by Ross Smith and Keith Smith.

Bauhaus school of architecture and design founded in Weimar, Germany, by architect Walter Gropius, a proponent of the modern International Style.

English philosopher Bertrand Russell imprisoned for pacifism.

*1919–22* Turkish War of Independence: Italian, French, and Greek forces expelled.

| | |
|---|---|
| *1920* | League of Nations formed. |
| | Kenya became a British colony. |
| | Start of Prohibition in USA: alcohol illegal. |
| | This led to widespread bootlegging and the Internal Revenue's loss was the crime syndicates' gain. |
| | Women achieved vote in USA. |
| | The chromosome theory of heredity was postulated by US geneticist Thomas H Morgan. |
| | The first regular radio broadcasts were made, in Detroit and Pittsburgh, USA. |
| | *Beyond the Horizon*, Eugene O'Neill's first play, marked the beginning of serious theatre in the USA. |
| *1921* | Insulin was first isolated from the pancreas by Canadian physicians Frederick Banting and Charles Best. |
| | Irish Free State created in S Ireland. |
| | Breakaway Chinese government set up under Sun Yat-sen. |
| *1922* | USSR formed. |
| | Joseph Stalin appointed general secretary of the Soviet Communist Party. |
| | Fascist Mussolini became prime minister in Italy. |

---

*For my part I prefer 50,000 rifles to 50,000 votes.*
**Benito Mussolini**
1921

---

Nominal end of British protectorate in Egypt; British troops remained.

Fascist coup in Bulgaria.

Kurdish rebellion put down by Royal Air Force bombardment. Tutankhamen's tomb in Egypt was opened by British archaeologist Howard Carter.

Austrian philosopher Ludwig Wittgenstein published *Tractatus Logico-Philosophicus*.

James Joyce's experimental novel *Ulysses* published in Paris.

**1923**    French and Belgian troops occupied the Ruhr Valley, Germany, in an attempt to force Germany to pay war reparations.

Turkish republic founded by Kemal Atatürk.

Palestine, Transjordan, and Iraq mandated to Britain; Syria to France.

Earthquake destroyed much of Tokyo and killed 99,000 people.

**1924**    USA limited immigration and barred Japanese, but gave citizenship to the remaining American Indians.

North Rhodesia became a British protectorate.

Death of Czech writer Franz Kafka, whose novels of nightmarish bureaucracy were published posthumously.

*Surrealist Manifesto* drawn up by French Dadaist André Breton.

The style drew on the Freudian concept of the unconscious, expressed in art (Salvador Dalí, René Magritte), poetry (Louis Aragon), and film

(Luis Buñuel).

**1925** Locarno Conference to ease tensions in Europe.

Independent Lebanon established.

Death of Sun Yat-sen; Chiang Kai-shek became commander in chief of the Guomindang forces.

British physicist Edward Appleton discovered a layer of the atmosphere that reflects radio waves; it was later named after him.

Latvian director Sergei Eisenstein's film *The Battleship Potemkin* released in USSR.

F Scott Fitzgerald's novel *The Great Gatsby* epitomized the US Jazz Age.

Louis Armstrong made his first records with the Hot Five.

Duke Ellington's Washingtonians also started recording.

---

*A lot of cats copy the Mona Lisa, but people still line up to see the original.*
**Louis Armstrong**
When asked whether he objected to people copying his style

---

**1926** General strike in UK in May, triggered by a cut in miners' wages.

Right-wing coup in Lithuania.

Military coup in Poland: nationalist former head of state Józef Pilsudski made himself dictator.

Swiss psychologist Jean Piaget presented his first book on child development.

Wave mechanics was introduced by Austrian

physicist Erwin Schrdinger.

US engineer Robert Goddard launched the first liquid-fuel rocket.

Scottish electrical engineer John Logie Baird demonstrated a workable television system.

---

*Already we Viewers, when not viewing, have begun to whisper to one another that the more we elaborate our means of communication, the less we communicate.*
**J B Priestley** On television
*The Writer in a Changing Society* 1957

---

US writer Ernest Hemingway published his first novel, *The Sun Also Rises*; his stripped-down style became highly influential.

*1927*

First Chinese communist uprising, in Nanchang; Chiang Kai-shek began purge of communists, who were now led by Mao Zedong.

The commercial production of polyacrylic polymers began.

The uncertainty principle of atomic physics was established by German physicist Werner Heisenberg.

US aviator Charles Lindbergh made the first W–E solo non-stop flight across the Atlantic.

Virginia Woolf's novel *To the Lighthouse*, using Modernist techniques, published in UK.

*The Jazz Singer*, the first feature film with an integrated soundtrack, released in USA.

Jerome Kern's *Showboat*, with libretto by Oscar

Hammerstein II, laid the foundations of the US musical.

**1928**     Kellogg-Briand pact condemning war.

Stalin emerged as Soviet dictator.

Antonio Salazar became dictator in Portugal.

In Britain all women over the age of 21 were granted the vote.

Scottish bacteriologist Alexander Fleming discovered penicillin.

Walt Disney released his first Mickey Mouse cartoon in USA.

---

*I love Mickey Mouse more than any woman I've ever known.*
**Walt Disney**

---

In Germany, Bertolt Brecht's *Die Dreigroschenoper/The Threepenny Opera* with score by Kurt Weill was their first collaboration.

**1929**     Wall Street stock-market crash in USA, 29 Oct precipitated the Great Depression.

Military dictatorship in Yugoslavia.

Building of French fortification system along German frontier, Maginot Line, began.

Soviet revolutionary Leon Trotsky ousted and forced into exile.

US astronomer Edwin Hubble discovered that the universe is expanding.

English sculptor Henry Moore made his first *Reclining Figure*.

| | |
|---|---|
| *1930* | One of a series of military coups in Argentina. |
| | Revolution created dictatorship in Brazil. |
| | The planet Pluto was located by Clyde Tombaugh at the Lowell Observatory, Arizona, USA. |
| | British engineer Frank Whittle patented the jet engine. |
| | British aviator Amy Johnson became the first woman to fly solo from England to Australia. |
| | German-born Marlene Dietrich became a star with the film *The Blue Angel*, directed by Josef von Sternberg. |
| | *The Maltese Falcon* by Dashiell Hammett introduced the hard-boiled detective into US fiction. |
| *1931* | Mukden Incident: surprise attack on Chinese garrison in Manchuria began the Japanese invasion of China. |
| | The cyclotron, a particle accelerator, was developed by US physicist Ernest Lawrence. |
| | US radio engineer Karl Jansky founded radio astronomy. |
| | Austrian-born mathematician Kurt Gödel proved that any formal system strong enough to include the laws of arithmetic is either incomplete or inconsistent. |
| | The then-tallest building in the world, Empire State Building, opened in New York. |
| *1932* | Saudi Arabia established. |
| | Japan created a puppet state, Manchukuo, in Manchuria (until 1945). |

The discovery of the neutron was made by British physicist James Chadwick.

The electron microscope was developed by Russian-born electronics engineer Vladimir Zworykin in the USA.

Charles Glen King isolated ascorbic acid (vitamin C).

1932–33    French artist Henri Matisse created mural *The Dance*.

1932–35    Chaco War between Paraguay and Bolivia.

1933       Nazis came to power in Germany; Adolf Hitler became chancellor.

The Nazis used the Reichstag (parliament building) fire, 27 Feb to justify the suspension of many constitutional guarantees.

Japan left League of Nations.

US president F D Roosevelt announced his New Deal to counter the Depression.

E W Fawcett and R O Gibson first produced polyethylene (polyethene/polythene) by the high-pressure polymerization of ethylene (ethene).

1934       Long March by Chinese communists began under Mao's leadership, harassed by Guomindang forces; 100,000 left Jianxi in Oct 1934 and only 8,000 arrived the following Oct in Shanxi, 10,000 km/6,000 mi away.

Artificial radioactivity was developed in France by Frédéric and Irène Joliot-Curie.

1934–38    Some 10 million people in USSR executed or deported to labour camps during Stalin's purges.

| | |
|---|---|
| *1935* | Burma separated from India. |
| | Philippines became self-governing. |
| | Ethiopia occupied by Italy. |
| | In Austria, Konrad Lorenz published the first of many studies of animal behaviour, which founded the discipline of ethology. |
| | US seismologist Charles Francis Richter established a scale for measuring the magnitude of earthquakes. |
| | US composer George Gershwin created the opera *Porgy and Bess*. |
| *1936* | Rome-Berlin Axis formed, allying Fascist Italy with Nazi Germany. |
| | Germany and Japan signed Anti-Comintern Pact, opposing communism as a menace to peace. |
| | Spanish Civil War began with right-wing revolt against government. |
| | Edward VIII, king of Great Britain and Northern Ireland, abdicated to enable him to marry a divorcée. |

---

*I have found it impossible to carry the heavy burden of responsibility and to discharge my duties as king as I would wish to do, without the help and support of the woman I love.*
**King Edward VIII**
Abdication speech on radio Dec 1936

---

The BBC began regular television broadcasts.

In the UK, Alan Turing published the

mathematical theory of computing.

English poet W H Auden, later a US citizen, published *Look, Stranger!*

**1937**     Japan invaded China.

Italy joined Anti-Comintern Pact.

The first fully pressurized aircraft, the Lockheed XC-35, came into service.

In Germany, Wernher von Braun developed the V2 rocket.

Wallace Carothers invented nylon.

Polyurethanes were first produced.

Geman-built airship Hindenburg exploded in USA.

Picasso painted *Guernica* in protest at the bombing of civilians in the Spanish Civil War.

Jean Renoir's antiwar film *La Grande Illusion* released in France.

New Bauhaus founded in Chicago, the original school having been closed by the Nazis 1933.

**1938**     Munich Agreement signed 29 Sept by the leaders of the UK, France, Germany, and Italy, under which Czechoslovakia was compelled to give up Sudetenland to Gemany.

Kristallnacht, 9–10 Nov: pogrom of Jews in Germany and Austria.

Konrad Zuse constructed the first binary calculator, using Boolean algebra.

Germany produced its 'people's car', the Volks-wagen Beetle.

Graham Greene's novel *Brighton Rock* published in UK.

*1939*          Italy conquered Albania.

Germany signed nonaggression pact with USSR.

USSR invaded Finland.

Germany invaded Czechoslovakia and Poland.

Start of World War II: UK declared war on 3
Sept.

---

*A racing tipster who only reached Hitler's level
of accuracy would not do well for his clients.*
**A J P Taylor**
*The Origins of the Second World War*

---

General Franco established a fascist dictatorship
in Spain.

The discovery of nuclear fission was made by
German chemists Otto Hahn and Fritz
Strassmann.

Erich Warsitz flew the first Heinkel jet plane, in
Germany.

In the USA, Igor Sikorsky designed the first
helicopter, with a large main rotor and a smaller
tail rotor.

An Anglo-Saxon ship-burial treasure was found
at Sutton Hoo, England.

*The Grapes of Wrath* by US novelist John
Steinbeck chronicled the hardships of migrant
farm workers leaving the Oklahoma dust bowl
for California.

| | |
|---|---|
| *1940* | Italy expelled from Somalia, Eritrea, and Ethiopia. |
| | Germany invaded France; Allied troops evacuated from Dunkirk beaches. |
| | Italy joined war against Allies. |
| | Battle of Britain, July–Oct, between Royal Air Force and German Luftwaffe. |
| | Germany began exterminating Jews. |
| | In the UK, German-born Hans Krebs proposed the citric acid (Krebs) cycle by which food molecules are converted into energy in living tissue. |
| | Edwin McMillan and Philip Abelson showed that new elements with a higher atomic number than uranium can be formed by bombarding uranium with neutrons, and synthesized the first transuranic element, neptunium. |
| | Lithium treatment for manic-depressive illness was developed. |
| | Walt Disney's *Fantasia* introduced classical music, conducted by Leopold Stokowski, to a worldwide audience of filmgoers. |
| *1941* | Japan began to overrun SE Asia and attacked the US naval base on Hawaii, Pearl Harbor, on 7 Dec; USA entered World War II. |
| | China joined Allies. |
| | Germany invaded USSR. |
| | World War II reached N Africa. |
| | Penicillin was isolated and characterized by Australian pathologist Howard Florey and British biochemist Ernst Chain. |

Orson Welles's landmark film *Citizen Kane* released in USA.

**1942**     Battle of El Alamein in the western desert of N Egypt between British field marshal Montgomery's 8th Army and German field marshal Rommel's forces.

Japan conquered Singapore.

Battle of Midway Islands: US naval victory marked turning point in Pacific War.

Battle of Stalingrad (now Volgograd), Aug–Nov; its successful defence against German onslaught determined the course of the war.

The first controlled nuclear chain reaction was achieved in USA by Italian-born Enrico Fermi.

---

*Whatever Nature has in store for mankind, unpleasant as it may be, man must accept, for ignorance is never better than knowledge.*
**Enrico Fermi**
*Atoms in the Family*

---

Plutonium was first synthesized by US chemist Glenn T Seaborg and US physicist Edwin McMillan.

*Nighthawks* by US painter Edward Hopper characteristically captured a mood of urban loneliness.

**1943**     Italy surrendered.

USSR drove Germans back.

End of Axis resistance in N Africa.

The role of DNA in genetic inheritance was first

demonstrated by Oswald Avery, Colin MacLeod, and Maclyn McCarty.

The industrial production of silicones was initiated.

J R Whinfield invented Terylene, the first wholly synthetic fibre created in the UK.

Humphrey Bogart and Ingrid Bergman starred in the romantic US film *Casablanca*.

**1944**    D-day Normandy landings by Allies 6 June.

Ho Chi Minh became president of independent Vietnam.

New plays included, in France, existentialist philosopher Jean-Paul Sartre's *Huis Clos/In Camera* and Jean Anouilh's Neo-Classical *Antigone*; in the USA, Arthur Miller's *Death of a Salesman*.

---

*Nobody has a more sacred obligation to obey the law than those who make the law.*
**Jean Anouilh**
*Antigone*

---

British painter Francis Bacon developed his distorted Expressionist style.

**1945**    Yalta Conference between Allied leaders.

United Nations (UN) formed; charter drawn up at San Francisco Conference.

Battle of Okinawa: 60,000 Japanese died unsuccessfully defending the island, which was then held by USA until 1972.

USA dropped atomic bombs on Hiroshima (6

Aug) and Nagasaki (9 Aug); Japan surrendered.

---

*We have resolved to endure the unendurable and suffer what is insufferable.*
**Emperor Hirohito of Japan**
On accepting the Allied terms of surrender, broadcasting to the nation Aug 1945

---

US and Soviet troops entered Korea.

End of World War II; start of Cold War.

Labour government elected in UK, began to establish welfare state.

Communist takeover in E Europe.

Civil war resumed in China.

Radar contact with the Moon was established by Z Bay of Hungary and the US Army Signal Corps Laboratory.

---

*The real danger is not that computers will begin to think like men, but that men will begin to think like computers.*
**S J Harris**
On the computer

---

The first general-purpose, fully electronic digital computer, ENIAC (electronic numerator, integrator, analyser, and computer), was built at the University of Pennsylvania, USA.

*1946*        Jordan and Philippines independent.

The first fast nuclear reactor built at Los Alamos, New Mexico.

US Abstract Expressionist Jackson Pollock invented action painting.

**1946–49** Greek Civil War: attempt to establish a socialist state suppressed by royalists with US aid.

**1947** India and Pakistan independent.

A rocket-powered plane, the Bell X-1, was the first aircraft to fly faster than the speed of sound.

US architect Buckminster Fuller invented the geodesic dome.

Southern US playwright Tennessee Williams wrote *A Streetcar Named Desire*.

---

*I can't stand a naked light bulb, any more than I can a rude remark or a vulgar action.*
**Tennessee Williams**
*A Streetcar Named Desire*

---

The first of the Dead Sea Scrolls, including ancient copies of Old Testament books, was discovered south of Jericho.

**1948** Apartheid began in South Africa.

Korea divided.

Burma and Ceylon (Sri Lanka) independent.

Israel established.

Organization of American States formed.

Marshall Plan of US aid for Europe.

Berlin blockade: the surrounding Soviet forces closed off West Berlin in June; Britain and USA responded by an airlift of supplies until the blockade was lifted May 1949.

William Shockley of Bell Laboratories, USA, invented the transistor.

The 5-m/200-in Hale reflector telescope was installed at Mount Palomar, California, USA.

**1J48–49** First Arab-Israeli War: Israel annexed more territory.

**1949** North Atlantic Treaty Alliance (NATO) formed.

People's Republic of China established under Mao Zedong.

Chiang Kai-shek set up Guomindang government on Taiwan.

Indonesia independent.

Germany divided into East and West.

Near civil war, La Violencia, began in Colombia, where 250,000 people were to die in political violence in the next decade.

Comecon, an East-bloc economic organization, formed.

English writer George Orwell published the political satire *Animal Farm*.

*La deuxième Sexe/The Second Sex* by Simone de Beauvoir, a classic feminist work, published in France.

| | |
|---|---|
| *1950* | Senator Joe McCarthy's anticommunist campaign began in the USA. |
| | Schuman Plan: French foreign minister proposed a common market for coal and steel that was to become the core of the European Community. |
| | Colombo Plan: international organization for economic development in S and SE Asia. |
| | Proof of a link between cigarette smoking and lung cancer was established. |
| | The basic components of DNA were established by Erwin Chargaff; the alphahelical structure of proteins was established by Linus Pauling and R B Corey in USA. |
| | Dunlop announced the disc brake. |
| | Antidepressant drugs and beta-blockers for heart disease were developed. |
| | Manipulation of the molecules of synthetic chemicals became the main source of new drugs. |
| | British immunologist Peter Medawar studied the body's tolerance of transplanted organs and skin grafts. |
| | Several early hominid fossils were found by Louis Leakey in Olduvai Gorge in Tanzania. |
| | Akira Kurosawa's *Rashōmon* was the first Japanese film shown in the West. |
| *1950–53* | Korean War: North Korea (supported by USSR) invaded South Korea (supported by USA under UN umbrella). |
| *1951* | Libya independent. |
| | China occupied Tibet. |

Japan signed treaties of peace with 49 nations.

First electricity generated by nuclear energy.

English composer Benjamin Britten's opera *Billy Budd* given premiere.

*1952*     End of Allied occupation of West Germany.

End of US occupation of Japan.

Greece and Turkey joined NATO.

Mau Mau campaign against colonists in Kenya.

De Haviland Comet offered world's first jet passenger service between London and Johannesburg.

US avant-garde composer John Cage staged the first *Happening* (one-off performance art).

---

*What I try to do in my plays is to get this recognizable reality of the absurdity of what we do and how we behave and how we speak.*
**Harold Pinter**
On the Theatre of the Absurd

---

*1953*     Death of Stalin in USSR.

Coup in Colombia.

Egypt became a republic.

Cambodia achieved independence from France.

Colour television broadcasting began in the USA.

James Watson and Francis Crick described the molecular structure of the genetic material, DNA.

B F Skinner's *Science of Human Behaviour*, a

text of operant conditioning, was published.

*En attendant Godot/Waiting for Godot* by Samuel Beckett exemplified the Theatre of the Absurd.

With Nepalese Sherpa Tenzing Norgay, New Zealand climber Edmund Hillary reached the summit of Mount Everest, the world's highest peak.

Inauguration of the city of Chandigarh, N India, designed by Swiss architect Le Corbusier.

*1954*     US-backed military coup in Guatemala halted nationalization and land reform.

Warsaw Pact formed: military alliance between USSR and Eastern European communist states.

West Germany joined NATO.

In the Battle of Dien Bien Phu in N Vietnam March–May, the communist Vietminh took a French fortress.

This marked the end of French control of Indochina.

Newly independent Vietnam was divided into North and South.

Conflict between the communist Vietcong in the S and the pro-Western government led to war.

Laos and Cambodia independent.

SEATO (Southeast Asian Treaty Organization) formed (to 1977).

Algerian War of Independence began.

English writer William Golding published his first novel, *Lord of the Flies*.

*Running has given me a glimpse of the greatest freedom a man can ever know because it results in the simultaneous liberation of both mind and body.*
**Roger Bannister**
*First Four Minutes*

Karlheinz Stockhausen's *Electronic Studies for magnetic tape* were broadcast in Cologne, Germany.

Edgard Varèse's *Déserts*, the first work to combine musical instruments and prerecorded magnetic tape, was performed in Paris.

Elvis Presley made his first rock-and-roll recordings in Memphis, Tennessee.

Jasper Johns's first *Flag* painting heralded Pop Art in USA.

English athlete Roger Bannister became the first person to run a mile in under four minutes.

*1954–58*     USA desegregated its public schools.

*1955*     Baghdad Pact (Iraq and Turkey, and later Persia).

Montgomery bus boycott in Alabama, led by Martin Luther King, was a landmark in the US civil-rights movement.

Russian-born Belgian chemist Ilya Prigogine des-cribed the thermodynamics of irreversible processes (the transformations of energy that take place in, for example, many reactions within living cells).

Artificial diamonds were first produced.

Vincent Du Vigneaud in USA made the first synthesis of a polypeptide hormone.

The first nuclear-powered submarine, *Nautilus*, was built in USA.

The hovercraft was patented by British inventor Christopher Cockerell.

---

*We are not at war with Egypt.*
*We are in an armed conflict.*
**Anthony Eden**
On the Suez Crisis

---

*1956*

Soviet troops crushed uprising in Hungary.

Polish riots against Soviet exploitation and food shortages.

Suez Crisis Oct–Dec: following the nationalization of the Suez Canal by Egypt's president Abdel Nasser, France and the UK intervened militarily. International criticism forced their withdrawal and the resignation of UK prime minister Eden.

Second Arab-Israeli War, another consequence of the Suez Crisis.

Morocco, Sudan, and Tunisia independent.

Coup attempt by Marxist revolutionaries Fidel Castro and Che Guevara against Cuban military dictator Fulgencio Batista.

The first transatlantic telephone cable was laid.

The neutrino, an elementary particle, was discovered by Clyde Cowan and Fred Reines.

US geologists Bruce Charles Heezen and

Maurice Ewing discovered a global network of oceanic ridges and rifts that divide the Earth's surface into plates.

Seagram Building, New York, designed in International Style by German architect Ludwig Mies van der Rohe.

Swedish director Ingmar Bergman made the complex metaphysical film *The Seventh Seal*.

---

*Neutrinos, they are very small./They have no charge and have no mass /And do not interact at all.*
**John Updike**
**On neutrinos**
*Cosmic Gall*

---

The first annual Warsaw Autumn Festival of contemporary music was held.

This became important for the promotion of Polish composers such as Witold Lutoslwski and Krzystof Penderecki.

The English Stage Company was formed at the Royal Court Theatre to provide a platform for new dramatists. John Osborne's *Look Back in Anger* was included in its first season.

*1957*   European Economic Community established by six countries through Treaty of Rome.

Ghana independent.

The Jodrell Bank telescope dish in England was completed.

The first Sputnik satellite (USSR) opened the

age of space observation.

German engineer Felix Wankel built his first rotary petrol engine.

Polish director Andrzej Wajda made the harrowing film of wartime Warsaw, *Kanal*.

Leonard Bernstein's musical *West Side Story* opened in New York.

**1958**   Alaska became a state of the USA.

Revolution in Iraq: monarchy overthrown by military.

Military coup in Pakistan.

Egypt and Syria formed United Arab Republic (to 1961).

The first integrated circuit was constructed.

Using rockets, US physicist James Van Allen discovered a belt of radiation (later named after him) around the Earth.

The structure of RNA (ribonucleic acid) was determined.

English obstetrician Ian Donald pioneered diagnostic ultrasound.

First European soccer championship held.

Brazilian footballer Pelé first appeared in a World Cup competition.

**1959**   China crushed uprising in Tibet, and had border clashes with India.

Cuban Revolution: Castro overthrew Batista.

Hawaii became a state of the USA.

The International Antarctic Treaty suspended all territorial claims, reserving an area south of

60°S latitude for peaceful purposes.

Pan-Africanist Congress broke from the ANC, arguing that only black people should rule South Africa.

The Mini car, designed in the UK by Alec Issigonis, introduced.

The Du Pont company developed Lycra.

The first nuclear-powered surface ship, the Soviet ice-breaker *Lenin*, was commissioned; the US *Savannah* became the first nuclear-powered merchant ship.

*USS Nautilus* made submerged crossing of North Pole.

The last work of US architect Frank Lloyd Wright was the Guggenheim Museum, New York, completed the year of his death.

Jean-Luc Godard's film *A Bout de souffle/ Breathless* popularized the French New Wave in cinema.

*1960*
Right-wing coup in Laos.

South Africa outlawed the ANC.

Sharpeville massacre: 69 anti-apartheid demonstrators killed in South Africa.

Central African Republic, Chad, Cyprus, Ivory Coast, Madagascar, Mali, Niger, Nigeria, Upper Volta (Burkina Faso), and Zaire independent.

The world's first weather satellite, TIROS 1, was launched.

A new generation of minor tranquillizers called benzodiazepines (Valium, Librium) was developed.

Harold Pinter's play *The Caretaker* was produced in London.

---

*One way of looking at speech is to say that it is a constant stratagem to cover nakedness.*
**Harold Pinter**

---

*1961*
Exiled Cuban rebels, trained and supplied by USA, made unsuccessful attempt to invade Cuba at Bay of Pigs.

Sierra Leone and Tanganyika independent.

South Africa became a republic, withdrawing from the Commonwealth.

Berlin Wall built.

The first crewed spaceship, Vostok 1 (USSR), with Yuri Gagarin on board, was recovered after a single orbit of 89.1 min at a height of 142,175 km/88,109 mi.

Meteorologist Edward Lorenz discovered a

mathematical system with chaotic behaviour, leading to a new branch of mathematics chaos theory.

Volcanic island of Tristan da Cunha erupted and population evacuated.

US actress Marilyn Monroe starred in her last film, *The Misfits*.

**1962**   Cuban missile crisis in Oct: confrontation between USA and USSR over the installation of Soviet missiles on Cuba threatened nuclear war.

Algeria, Jamaica, Trinidad, and Uganda independent.

US U-2 spy plane shot down over USSR and pilot Gary Powers imprisoned.

Sino-Indian border clashes.

The first X-ray source in outer space was discovered in the constellation Scorpius.

Benoit Mandelbrot in the USA invented fractal images, programming a computer to repeat the same mathematical pattern over and over again.

John Glenn in *Friendship 7* (USA) became the first American to orbit the Earth.

*Telstar*, a US communications satellite, sent the first live television transmission between the USA and Europe.

The publication of *Silent Spring* by US naturalist Rachel Carson drew public attention to the cumulative effects of pesticides on the environment.

**1963**   Organization of African Unity formed.

Kenya and Malaysia independent.

French vetoed British application to join EEC.

Nuclear Test Ban Treaty signed by USA, USSR, and Britain, agreeing to test nuclear weapons only underground.

France and China continued ground-level and underwater tests.

US president John F Kennedy assassinated, 22 Nov.

Martin Luther King led massive march on Washington DC to demand racial equality.

Valentina Tereshkova in *Vostok 6* (USSR) became the first woman in space.

The first minicomputer was built by Digital Equipment (DEC).

The first electronic calculator was built by Bell Punch Company.

Leslie Phillips and co-workers at the Royal Aircraft Establishment, Farnborough, England, invented carbon fibre.

Theodore Maiman developed the first laser.

The first quasar (small distant starlike object) was discovered.

Walter Emery pioneered rescue archaeology at Abu Simbel, Egypt, before the site was flooded by the Aswan Dam.

Yugoslavian city of Skopje destroyed by earthquake.

The Beatles' first LP released in UK; the start of Beatlemania.

*1964*     Malawi, Malaysia, Malta, and Zambia independent.

> *The inability of those in power to still the voices
> of their own consciences is the great force
> leading to change.*
> **Kenneth Kaunda,** first president of Zambia
> *Observer* July 1965

Tanzania founded by union of Tanganyika and Zanzibar.

Nelson Mandela and other ANC leaders imprisoned in South Africa.

Nikita Khrushchev ousted from Soviet leadership.

Greek-Turkish tension over Cyprus.

Palestine Liberation Organization (PLO) formed.

War between Indonesia and Malaysia.

Launch of IBM System/360, the first compatible family of computers.

Murray Gell-Mann and George Zweig in USA discovered the quark, an elementary particle.

Japan National Railways inaugurated the Shinkansen, or bullet train, between Osaka and Tokyo, with speed of 210 kph/130 mph.

English artist David Hockney made his first painting of a swimming pool.

Muhammad Ali (then called Cassius Clay) of USA became world heavyweight boxing champion.

*1965*          Ian Smith, white segregationist prime minister of colonial Rhodesia (from 1964), unilaterally declared independence from Britain, having already banned the nationalist opposition.

The Gambia independent.

Singapore seceded from the Federation of Malaysia.

US marines entered Vietnam.

US marines invaded the Dominican Republic.

India and Pakistan at war over Kashmir.

Insulin was first synthesized.

The psychedelic drug LSD (lysergic acid diethylamide) banned in USA (UK 1966).Robert Moog invented a synthesizer that considerably widened the scope of electronic music.

The soundtrack of the film *The Sound of Music*, with music by Rodgers and lyrics by Hammerstein, was released, and stayed in the sales charts for the next two years.

US songwriter Bob Dylan released *Highway 61 Revisited*.

**1966**  Botswana, Guyana, and Lesotho independent.

France left NATO.

Cultural Revolution in China began: artists and academics harassed by young Red Guards.

Militant Black Panther Party formed in USA.

Oil discovered beneath North Sea.

Specially protected areas were established internationally for animals and plants.

California introduced legislation to limit air pollution by cars.

The Velvet Underground avant-garde rock group

collaborated on multimedia shows with Pop artist Andy Warhol in New York.

**1967** Six-day Arab-Israeli War resulted in Israeli expansion.

State of Biafra declared independence from Nigeria, but was re-annexed in a war that cost a million lives and lasted until 1970.

Military coup in Greece.

Che Guevara killed in Bolivia.

The worst oil spill in British waters caused by the Torrey Canyon.

Christiaan Barnard performed the first human heart-transplant operation.

Vladimir Komarov was the first person to be killed in space research, when his ship, *Soyuz 1* (USSR), crash-landed on the Earth.

The first pulsar was discovered by British astronomers Jocelyn Bell and Antony Hewish.

Abortion Law Reform Act in UK put an end to back-street abortions.

LP *Are You Experienced?* by US guitarist Jimi Hendrix widened the scope of the instrument.

Tom Stoppard's play *Rosencrantz and Guildenstern are Dead* was produced at the Old Vic Theatre, London.

Colombian novelist Gabriel García Márquez published the magic-realist *Cien años de soledad/One Hundred Years of Solitude.*

**1968** Prague Spring of liberalization in Czechoslovakia suppressed by Warsaw Pact troops on Soviet orders in Aug.

Mauritius independent.

Tet Offensive in Vietnam: prolonged attack by Vietcong on Saigon.

My Lai massacre of civilians by US troops.

Martin Luther King assassinated.

---

*I have a dream that my four little children will one day live in a nation where they will not be judged by the color of their skin but by the content of their character.*
**Martin Luther King**
Speech Washington DC June 1963

---

Violence in Northern Ireland: start of the Troubles.

The world's first supersonic airliner, the Russian TU-144, flew for the first time.

Abolition of theatre censorship in the UK.

Baader-Meinhof gang began direct action in Europe against what they perceived as US imperialism.

---

*As for the Yankees, they have no other ambition than to take possession of this new continent of the sky [the Moon] and to plant upon the summit of its highest elevation the star-spangled banner of the United States.*
**Jules Verne**
On space travel 1865

---

Libyan revolution: king deposed by Moamer

al-Khaddhafi making it a one-party Islamic socialist state.

US bombing raids on neutral Cambodia began.

The first Moon landing was made by US astronauts.

Neil Armstrong of *Apollo 11* (USA) was the first person to walk on the Moon, 20 July.

| | |
|---|---|
| **1970** | Salvador Allende became president of Chile, the world's first democratically elected Marxist head of state. |
| | Prince Sihanouk of Cambodia overthrown by US-backed Lon Nol. |
| | *Luna 17* (USSR) was launched; its space probe, *Lunokhod*, took photographs and made soil analyses of the Moon's surface. |
| | The Boeing 747 jumbo jet entered service, carrying 500 passengers. |
| **1971** | East Pakistan seceded to become Bangladesh. |
| | China joined UN. |
| | Environmental pressure groups Greenpeace and Friends of the Earth formed. |
| | Superconductivity was proposed in theory – that electrical resistance in some metals vanishes at very low temperatures. |
| | The first microprocessor, the Intel 4004, was announced. |
| | Viroids, disease-causing organisms even smaller than viruses, were isolated outside the living body. |
| | *Salyut 1* (USSR), the first orbital space station, was established. |
| **1972** | Sri Lanka independent. |
| | Uganda expelled citizens of Asian origin. |
| | British direct rule introduced in Northern Ireland after British army killed 13 demonstrators. |
| | SALT I accord signed by USA and USSR, calling for a limit on the expansion of nuclear forces. |

The CAT scan, pioneered by Godfrey Hounsfield, was first used to image the human brain.

Bob Marley's LP *Catch a Fire* began popularization of reggae beyond Jamaica.

At the Olympics in Munich, W Germany, a Palestinian guerrilla group killed Israeli athletes; Soviet gymnast Olga Korbut won three gold medals.

*1973*    US-backed military coup in Chile; death of Allende.

Britain, Ireland, and Denmark entered EEC.

US troops left war-devastated Vietnam.

Arab-Israeli (Yom Kippur) War.

Oil prices raised, triggering worldwide recession.

Helsinki Conference on Security and Co-operation in Europe.

*Skylab 2*, the first US orbital space station, was established.

US film director Martin Scorsese hit his stride with *Mean Streets*.

*1973–74*    Three-day working week in UK necessitated by miners' strike.

*1974*    Portuguese dictatorship overthrown.

Partition of Cyprus.

IRA extended its bombing campaign to British mainland.

Watergate scandal in USA (began 1972) led to downfall of President Nixon.

*There can be no whitewash at the White House.*
**Richard Nixon**
Speech on Watergate

'White Australia' immigration policy abolished.

CLIP4, the first computer with a parallel architecture, was developed by John Backus at IBM.

The footprints of a hominid called 'Lucy', 3 to 3.7 million years old, were found at Laetoli in Ethiopia.

*1975*  Monarchy restored in Spain on death of Franco.

Portuguese colonies, including Mozambique and Angola, gained independence.

Civil war in Angola.

Surinam independent; 40% of population emigrated to Netherlands.

In Cambodia, Lon Nol overthrown by Pol Pot's Khmer Rouge; Phnom Penh forcibly evacuated.

End of Vietnam War; Saigon fell to Vietcong in April.

Start of civil war in Lebanon.

One-party communist republic proclaimed in Laos.

Papua New Guinea gained independence from Australia.

*Apollo 18* (USA) and *Soyuz 19* (USSR) made a joint flight and linked up in space.

Discovery of endogenous opiates (the brain's own painkillers) opened up a new phase in the study of brain chemistry.

Altair 8800, the first personal computer (PC), or microcomputer, was launched.

*1976*     Portugal held first free elections in 50 years.

Soweto riots in South Africa sparked by ruling that Afrikaans should be used in African schools.

North and South Vietnam reunited as socialist republic.

East Timor (in the Malay archipelago), which had declared independence on Portugal's withdrawal, was forcibly annexed by Indonesia.

Anglo-French aeroplane Concorde, making a transatlantic crossing in under three hours, came into commercial service.

Chinese city of Tangshan destroyed by earthquake; more than 200,000 killed.

Har Gobind Khorana and his colleagues constructed the first artificial gene to function naturally when inserted into a bacterial cell, a major step in genetic engineering.

Punk rock arrived with the Sex Pistols' *Anarchy in the UK*; punk style soon became global youth culture.

*1977*     Military coup in Pakistan.

Israel settled on West Bank.

Civil-rights leader Steve Biko died in custody of South African police.

Uranus was discovered to have rings.

The spacecrafts *Voyager 1* and 2 were launched by USA, passing Jupiter and Saturn 1979–1981.

The first fibreoptic telecommunications cable was laid, in California.

**1978** Camp David agreement on peace in the Middle East.

Israel invaded S Lebanon.

Military junta seized power in Afghanistan.

World's first test-tube baby (from fertilization outside the body) was born in the UK.

Human insulin was first produced by genetic engineering.

The spacecrafts *Pioneer Venus 1* and *2* reached Venus.

*Amoco Cadiz* ran aground off Brittany; 220 tonnes of oil spilled into sea.

Compact discs were first demonstrated.

Red Brigades kidnapped and killed former Italian prime minster Aldo Moro.

Right-wing *agents provocateurs* were subsequently blamed.

**1978–79** Winter of discontent in UK: a series of strikes brought down the Labour government.

Khmer Rouge in Cambodia ousted by Vietnamese.

**1979** Soviet invasion of Afghanistan, installing puppet government; Soviet troops and government forces opposed by mujaheddin Muslim guerrilla groups in long civil war.

Chinese briefly invaded Vietnam.

Margaret Thatcher became UK prime minister after Conservative electoral victory.

Sandinistas overthrew right-wing dictator

Anastasio Somoza in Nicaragua.

Islamic revolution in Iran, led by Ayatollah Khomeini; shah exiled.

Egypt and Israel signed peace treaty; Israel agreed to withdraw from Sinai peninsula.

Nuclear-reactor accident at Three Mile Island, Pennsylvania, USA.

The European Space Agency's satellite launcher, *Ariane 1*, was launched.

The Aztec capital Tenochtitln was excavated beneath a zone of Mexico City.

Japan National Railways' maglev test vehicle ML-500 attained a speed of 517 kph/321 mph.

Soviet director Andrei Tarkovsky made the allegorical film *Stalker*.

Rap music emerged in New York; it would become one of the dominant pop music styles of the next decade.

*1980*  A national confederation of independent trade unions, Solidarity, formed in Poland.

---

*It is one of the characteristics of a free and democratic modern nation that it have free and independent labor unions.*
**Franklin D Roosevelt** on trade unions
Speech Sept 1940

---

Zimbabwe (Rhodesia) independent.

Start of Iran–Iraq War, in which 1 million people were to die.

The World Health Organization reported the eradication of smallpox.

AIDS (acquired immune-deficiency syndrome) was first recognized in the USA.

Japanese car production overtook that of the USA.

Launch of the first wind-assisted commercial ship for half a century, the Japanese tanker *Shin-Aitoku-Maru.*

Mount St Helens in Washington State, USA, erupted and devasted an area of 600 sq km/230 sq mi.

*1981*  President Sadat of Egypt assassinated.

Greece joined European Community (EC).

Republican Ronald Reagan, a former film actor, became president of the USA.

The first reusable crewed spacecraft, the US space shuttle *Columbia*, was launched.

MTV (Music Television) started broadcasting

nonstop pop videos on cable in the USA.

The first graphical user-interface system (Xerox Star) for computers was developed.

IBM launched the IBM PC.

France's Train Grande à Vitesse (TGV) superfast trains began operation between Paris and Lyons, regularly attaining a peak speed of 270 kph/168 mph.

*1982*    Spain joined NATO.

Falklands War between Britain and Argentina.

---

*The Falklands thing was a fight between two bald men over a comb.*
**Jorge Luis Borges**
**On Falkland Islands War**
in *Time* 1983

---

Israel invaded Lebanon.

Palestinians massacred in Sabra-Chatila refugee camps.

Element 109, unnilennium, synthesized in Germany.

Gene databases were established in Heidelberg, Germany, for the European Molecular Biology Laboratory, and at Los Alamos, New Mexico, for the US National Laboratories.

The English king Henry VIII's warship *Mary Rose* of 1545 was raised.

*1983*    USA invaded Grenada.

First US cruise missiles deployed in Europe.

The virus responsible for AIDS, human

immuno-deficiency virus (HIV), was identified by Luc Montagnier at the Institut Pasteur, Paris; Robert Gallo at the National Cancer Institute, Maryland, USA, discovered the virus independently 1984.

The first commercially available product of genetic engineering (Humulin) was launched.

Evidence of the existence of weakons (W and Z particles) was confirmed at European nuclear laboratory of CERN, validating the link between the weak nuclear force and the electromagnetic force.

**1984**

About 2,600 people died in Bhopal, central India, when poisonous methyl isocyanate gas escaped from a chemical plant owned by US company Union Carbide.

UK affirmed agreement to return Hong Kong to China in 1997.

Ethiopian famine sparked worldwide aid effort.

Australian Aboriginal culture given legal protection.

French philosopher Michel Foucault, who analysed the structure of power in society, died.

A vaccine against leprosy was developed.

Apple launched the Macintosh computer.

**1985**

Mikhail Gorbachev came to power in USSR.

Japan became the world's largest creditor nation.

Fullerenes, a new class of carbon solids made of closed cages of carbon atoms, were discovered by Harold Kroto and David Walton at the University of Sussex, England.

British geneticist Alec Jeffreys devised genetic fingerprinting.

The first human cancer gene, retinoblastoma, was isolated by researchers in Massachusetts, USA.

A British expedition to the Antarctic discovered a hole in the ozone layer above the South Pole.

**1986**     Irangate scandal broke in USA, revealing secret arms-for-hostages trade with Iran and illicit funding of Nicaraguan Contras.

Spain and Portugal joined EC.

USA bombed Libya.

Overthrow of President Ferdinand Marcos in Philippines by nonviolent populist movement; Corazon Aquino elected.

Gorbachev introduced *perestroika* (reform) and *glasnost* (openness) in the USSR.

Accident at Chernobyl reactor in Ukraine killed 250 people and contaminated thousands of square kilometres.

Big Bang: de-regulation of the London Stock Exchange.

The International Whaling Commission (IWC) agreed to ban commercial whaling.

The first high-temperature superconductor was discovered, able to conduct electricity without resistance at a temperature of 35K.

Space shuttle *Challenger* (USA) exploded shortly after take-off, killing all seven crew members.

*Voyager 2* flew past Uranus and discovered six

new moons.

Viv Richards became captain of the West Indies cricket team.

*1987*   USA and USSR signed Intermediate Nuclear Forces Treaty to reduce the number of ground-based missiles.

Intifada (Palestinian uprising) began in Gaza in Dec and spread to the other Israeli-occupied territories.

Black Monday 19 Oct: worldwide stock-market crash.

France and the UK began work on the Channel Tunnel, a railway link running beneath the English Channel.

Supernova SN1987A flared up, becoming the first supernova to be visible to the naked eye since 1604.

US chemists Donald Cram and Charles Pederson, and Jean-Marie Lehn of France, created artificial molecules that mimic the vital chemical reactions of life processes.

*1988*   Estonia, Latvia, and Lithuania moved towards independence.

Benazir Bhutto became prime minister of Pakistan and the world's first female leader of a Muslim state.

USA became the world's largest debtor nation, owing $532 billion.

Terrorist bombing of US airliner over Lockerbie, Scotland, blamed on Libya.

*Daedelus*, a human-powered craft piloted by

Kanellos Kanellopoulos, flew 118 km/74 mi across the Aegean Sea.

The first optical microprocessor, which uses light instead of electricity, was developed.

The Human Genome Organization (HUGO) was established in Washington DC with the aim of mapping the complete sequence of DNA.

The most distant individual star was recorded, a supernova, 5 billion light years away, in the AC118 cluster of galaxies.

Soviet space shuttle Buran was launched from the rocket *Energiya*.

Soviet cosmonauts Musa Manarov and Vladimir Titov in space station Mir spent a record 365 days 59 min in space.

Videophones introduced in Japan.

Earthquake in Armenia killed 100,000.

*1989*    Cold War declared over (Nov).

Soviet troops left Afghanistan.

Pro-democracy demonstrations in China crushed; students massacred in Tiananmen Square, Beijing.

Republican George Bush became US president.

USA invaded Panama.

Berlin Wall opened.

Revolutions in Eastern Europe against communist rule.

Vietnamese military withdrawal from Cambodia complete; civil war intensified.

Death threats by Islamic groups against British writer Salman Rushdie, his translators and publishers, for the allegedly blasphemous content of his 1988 novel *The Satanic Verses*.

*Voyager 2* flew by Neptune and discovered eight moons and three rings.

Grafts of fetal brain tissue were first used to treat Parkinson's disease.

High-definition television introduced in Japan.

Oil tanker *Exxon Valdez* ran aground in Prince William Sound, Alaska; 40 million litres of oil spilled.

Second San Francisco earthquake.

US film director Spike Lee tackled New York's ethnic unrest in *Do the Right Thing*.

**1990**    Dismantling of apartheid in South Africa began;
Nelson Mandela released in Feb.

---

*I have cherished the idea of a democratic and
free society . if needs be, it is an ideal for which I
am prepared to die.*
**Nelson Mandela**
Speech on South Africa Feb 1990

---

Namibia independent.

Civil war in Liberia.

Iraq invaded Kuwait.

Germany reunified.

Free elections in Hungary, Romania, Bulgaria,
and Czechoslovakia.

First democratic elections in Haiti.

Riots against the poll tax in UK.

Thatcher forced to resign; John Major became
British prime minister.

Unification of North and South Yemen.

Burmese elections won by Aung San Suu Kyi,
who was placed under house arrest by military
dictatorship.

Gene for maleness discovered by UK
researchers.

Microsoft released Windows 3, a popular
graphical user interface for PCs.

There were 550 million motor vehicles on the
world's roads.

Czech-US tennis player Martina Navratilova

won her ninth Wimbledon singles title.

Gulf War, 16 Jan–28 Feb: mostly US forces under UN umbrella forced Iraq to withdraw from Kuwait.

Soviet troops sent into Lithuania and Latvia (Jan) and Estonia (Aug).

Bank of Commerce and Credit International shut down for fraud and money-laundering.

Military coup in Haiti.

Civil war in Yugoslavia.

Boris Yeltsin elected president of Soviet Union's Russian Republic. Failed coup against Gorbachev in Aug; he resigned in Dec with the dissolution of the USSR. Constituent republics became independent states.

---

*The policy prevailed of dismembering this country and disuniting the state, with which I cannot agree.*
**Mikhail Gorbachev**
Resignation speech 25 Dec 1991

---

Warsaw Pact disbanded.

Indian Congress Party leader Rajiv Gandhi assassinated.

Indonesian troops massacred demonstrators in East Timor.

Canada reached agreement with Inuit over land claim.

Mystery death of media tycoon Robert Maxwell led to discovery that he had plundered more than

£567 million from his company's pension fund.

Confirmation hearings of US Supreme Court nominee Clarence Thomas generated international debate about sexual harassment.

AIDS victims worldwide numbered about 1 million, with 8–10 million infected with HIV.

The Antarctic Treaty imposing a 50-year ban on mining activity was secured.

The Gamma Ray Observatory was launched to survey the sky at gamma-ray wavelengths.

First successful use of gene therapy (to treat severe combined immune deficiency) was reported in the USA.

IBM developed world's fastest high-capacity memory computer chip, SRAM (static random access memory), able to send or receive 8 billion bits of information per second.

Superconducting salts of buckminster fullerene were discovered by researchers at AT & T Bell Laboratories, New Jersey, USA.

Biosphere 2, an experiment that attempted to reproduce the world's biosphere in miniature within a sealed glass dome, was launched in Arizona, USA.

Body of man from 5,300 years ago, with clothing, bow, arrows, a copper axe, and other implements, found preserved in Italian Alps.

*1992*          Yugoslavia broke up amid civil war.

Black Wednesday 16 Sept: UK dropped out of the European Monetary System, effectively devaluing the pound, after spending est. £11–14 billion trying to prop it up.

Rio de Janeiro, Brazil, hosted Earth Summit, international conference on the environment.

EC crisis over Maastricht Treaty, concerning preconditions for closer unification.

Muslims replaced communists to rule Afghanistan.

South Africa voted for majority rule; continued unrest.

Civil war and famine in Somalia: US military intervention under UN umbrella.

Rioting in India between Muslims and Hindus began in Ayodhya and spread nationwide, killing hundreds.

Rioting erupted in Los Angeles, California, after white city police officers were acquitted of beating black motorist Rodney King.

They were later retried.

The violence killed 58 people and caused $1 billion worth of damages.

Philips launched the CD-I (compact disc-interactive) player, based on CD audio technology, to provide interactive multimedia programs for the home user.

Japanese researchers developed a material that becomes superconducting at −103°C/−153°F (about 45°C/80°F warmer than the previous record).

Blue-light-emitting diodes based on the organic chemical poly (p-phenylene) were reported by Australian researchers.

The world's largest organism, a honey fungus

with underground hyphae (filaments) spreading across 600 hectares/1,480 acres, was discovered in Washington State, USA.

Japanese propellerless ship *Yamato* driven by magneto-hydrodynamics completed its sea trials. The ship uses magnetic forces to suck in and eject sea water like a jet engine.

European satellite *Hipparcos*, launched 1989 to measure the position of 120,000 stars, failed to reach geostationary orbit. The mission was later retrieved.

COBE satellite detected ripples from the Big Bang that mark the first stage in the formation of galaxies.

*1993* Palestine Liberation Organization recognized Israel's right to exist; Israel agreed to Palestinian self-government and demilitarization of the occupied territories.

Czechoslovakia split into two: Czech Republic and Slovakia.

USA and Russia signed SALT II treaty to reduce nuclear arsenals.

Democrat Bill Clinton, former Arkansas governor, became US president and proposed health-care reforms.

---

*There is nothing wrong with America that cannot be cured by what is right with America.*
**Bill Clinton**
Inaugural speech as US President

---

Boris Yeltsin dissolved Russian parliament and

banned sections of the press.

Prince Sihanouk returned to Cambodia as constitutional monarch.

Fighting continued among Serb, Croat, and Muslim factions in Bosnia.

Civil war in Angola.

Eritrea, Macedonia, and Monaco became members of the UN.

Mafia-related scandals destabilized Italian government.

North Korea withdrew from the Nuclear Non-proliferation Treaty.

Change of government in Japan: the right-wing party that had been in power since 1955 was voted out in favour of a centrist coalition.

Nelson Mandela called for an end to the trade and consumer boycotts on South Africa.

Zaire close to anarchy and bankruptcy.

Tanker *Braer* spilled 100 million litres of oil off the Shetland Islands.

Norway defied the IWC ban and resumed commercial whaling.

US director Steven Spielberg's fantasy *Jurassic Park* became the highest-grossing film in history.

Chris Hani, secretary general of the South African Communist Party and a prominent ANC leader, assassinated.

Massive bomb exploded in a garage below the World Trade Center, New York City, killing five people.

US President George Bush and Russian President Boris Yeltsin signed the second Strategic Arms Reduction Treaty (START) in Moscow.

Russian scientists unfurled a giant mirror in orbit and flashed a beam of sunlight across Europe during the night.

Results of the Grand National steeplechase were voided because of starting problems. The fiasco was described as one of the most embarassing incidents in British sporting history.

In the UK, Beverly Allitt, a nurse, was sentenced to 13 life terms for the murders of four children in her care and attacks on nine others.

Italians voted in a referendum to support measures calling for government reform, amid an ever-growing political corruption scandal.

Russian President Yeltsin won 58 per cent support from voters participating in a country-wide referendum.

In Italy, a car bomb exploded near the Uffizi Gallery, Florence, killing five people, destroying three paintings, and damaging 30 others.

In the USA, compound of the Branch Davidians, a religious cult near Waco, Texas, burned to the ground, in what the FBI described as a mass suicide, killing at least 72 people.

Australian Labour Party, led by the prime minister, Paul Keating, won an unprecedented fifth consecutive three-year term in national elections.

EC's Maastricht Treaty ratified.